NEW DIRECTIONS FOR HIGHER EDUCATION

Martin Kramer
EDITOR-IN-CHIEF

D1028231

Developing Administrative Excellence: Creating a Culture of Leadership

Sharon A. McDade
Columbia University

Phyllis H. Lewis
University of Pennsylvania

EDITORS

Number 87, Fall 1994

JOSSEY-BASS PUBLISHERS
San Francisco

DEVELOPING ADMINISTRATIVE EXCELLENCE:
CREATING A CULTURE OF LEADERSHIP
Sharon A. McDade, Phyllis H. Lewis (eds.)
New Directions for Higher Education, no. 87
Volume XXII, Number 3
Martin Kramer, Editor-in-Chief

Microfilm copies of issues and articles are available in 16mm and 35mm, as well as microfiche in 105mm, through University Microfilms Inc., 300 North Zeeb Road, Ann Arbor, Michigan 48106-1346.

LC 85-644752   ISSN 0271-0560   ISBN 0-7879-9986-5

NEW DIRECTIONS FOR HIGHER EDUCATION is part of The Jossey-Bass Higher and Adult Education Series and is published quarterly by Jossey-Bass Inc., Publishers, 350 Sansome Street, San Francisco, California 94104-1342 (publication number USPS 990-880). Second-class postage paid at San Francisco, California, and at additional mailing offices. POST-MASTER: Send address changes to New Directions for Higher Education, Jossey-Bass Inc., Publishers, 350 Sansome Street, San Francisco, California 94104-1342.

SUBSCRIPTIONS for 1994 cost $47.00 for individuals and $62.00 for institutions, agencies, and libraries.

EDITORIAL CORRESPONDENCE should be sent to the Editor-in-Chief, Martin Kramer, 2807 Shasta Road, Berkeley, California 94708-2011.

Cover photograph and random dot by Richard Blair/Color & Light © 1990.

Manufactured in the United States of America. Nearly all Jossey-Bass books, jackets, and periodicals are printed on recycled paper that contains at least 50 percent recycled waste, including 10 percent postconsumer waste. Many of our materials are also printed with vegetable-based inks; during the printing process these inks emit fewer volatile organic compounds (VOCs) than petroleum-based inks. VOCs contribute to the formation of smog.

CONTENTS

Editors' Notes

Developing leaders for all segments of society through education has been one of the historic roles of American colleges and universities. In this era of lifelong learning, colleges and universities have created a multitude of executive and continuing education programs to develop leaders for new fields and to enhance the skills of people already in significant leadership positions. The amount of time, energy, and resources—particularly financial resources—invested in leadership development through college and university programming is staggering.

Unfortunately, the culture of higher education does not encourage this same investment in the leadership development of its own people. There is a pervasive attitude that leaders naturally rise to positions, that when new leadership is needed, it will be found through a search, and that the leader from outside an institution is always superior to the homegrown contender. These biases are magnified during tough economic times. When campuses are troubled financially, as many are in the 1990s, morale is often low and the tendency to polarize is greater. In the urgency to downsize and reengineer, homegrown leadership development is typically one of the first casualties.

In such times, an institutional awareness of the problems at hand is crucially needed. Turning around an institution in trouble and capitalizing on its strengths generally requires a change in attitudes and behavior. At such times, leadership of one or several individuals is not enough. A culture of leadership is needed.

Knowing exactly how to inspire and create a leadership culture can be difficult. Many institutions use the many national leadership development programs. Although the cumulative impact of these programs can be significant to an institution that regularly sends its people to attend, the greatest immediate benefits are to the individual. It takes a great deal of coordination and follow-up to extend those cumulative benefits to the campus as a whole, and few institutions make the effort to recoup these individual benefits in an organized way.

An approach that is gaining importance as a parallel leadership development effort and sometimes as a substitute for individual participation in national programs is the design of campus-based programs for faculty and staff. These programs acknowledge the potential contribution that current personnel can make to the institution and represent an institutional commitment toward developing that potential for the future.

The investment by higher education in the development of new leaders is a responsible approach that will ensure the viability of institutions and the entire system of American higher education. On-campus leadership development programming is a fiscally and academically sound response to the need for leadership development. Some universities have made commendable efforts, and are reaping the benefits of a leadership culture. This volume focuses on describing how various types of campus-based leadership programs work and how they can be replicated by other institutions.

Chapter One describes the need to create a culture of leadership in higher education to meet current challenges and to develop human resources for the future. It points out that some institutions have begun to reevaluate their commitment to staff development even in times of economic downsizing.

Chapter Two describes several variations on a traditional model of professional development: the internship. Individuals are selected for term assignments of a few weeks or months, some up to one academic year. Many of the current arrangements involve job rotations and exchanges. The primary goal is to provide mentoring experiences and expose individuals to different perspectives and experiences.

Developing institutional teams, as described in Chapter Three, may be the epitome of the leadership culture concept. The university sponsors the participation of groups of key personnel (usually senior administrators) in off-campus programs with the expectation that the close-knit experience, together with follow-up efforts, will enhance teamwork.

Chapter Four describes initiatives by some institutions that offer on-site programming aimed at improving management and leadership of key personnel and developing administrators. One goal from the institutions' perspective is to bring more players into solving institutional problems. From the participants' perspective, such experiences can provide more certain paths to future positions of leadership.

Some institutions within multicampus systems, consortia, networks, and associations jointly sponsor leadership development programs. These are described in Chapter Five. The institutions benefit from the shared pool of resources and development opportunities while providing development opportunities for a larger number of faculty and staff than any one institution could serve by itself. The systems and consortia also benefit through cross-pollination of ideas and employees.

Over the past ten years, many universities have managed to build good training programs, usually as part of their human resource or faculty development programs. Often these provide an important introduction for first-line and mid-level managers to principles of leadership and create a level of awareness for the campus that, in turn, can inspire senior leadership development. Several examples of staff development programs are described in Chapter Six.

Chapter Seven discusses how universities have responded to the need for leadership and staff development activities as the result of or as part of the quality improvement movement in higher education.

Chapter Eight investigates how institutions assess their leadership development programming, including the problems and benefits of such evaluation.

Chapter Nine makes the point that integration of leadership development programs into the life of the institution is the key to the long-term success of such activities. Otherwise, much of the real value, at least from the institutional perspective, is lost. On most campuses, that integration will represent a change in the way leadership is conceptualized and will probably produce some changes in the way institutional business is done.

Although these chapters present important models of leadership development that can be replicated at other institutions, points about their patterns of organization, financing, staffing, and content provide many ideas and opportunities for the development of other, better models of programming. These materials also suggest the need for further research on the scope and variety of existing programs and on how they really affect higher education.

Sharon A. McDade
Phyllis H. Lewis
Editors

SHARON A. McDADE is assistant professor of higher education and principal adviser of the higher education administration graduate programs at Teachers College, Columbia University.

PHYLLIS H. LEWIS is director of human resources at the University of Pennsylvania.

In financially troubled times, leadership by individuals is not enough; the campus must develop a culture of leadership.

Creating a Culture of Leadership

Phyllis H. Lewis

Leadership development programming can significantly strengthen the institution by fostering a team approach to solving institutional problems, by increasing the effectiveness and efficiency of its human resources, and by creating a ready pool of qualified professionals for top-level positions.

The many new books on higher education and conferences for major associations of college and university administrators point to a surge of interest within academia in the topic of leadership development. Much of this interest may be inspired by the proliferation in the popular press of commentary about leadership. Business school professors who formerly wrote mainly for themselves now have wide following among the general public. Although there is considerable fascination with the characteristics and genesis of leadership, there is also distrust, and often we are disappointed in our leaders. We tend to expect leaders to fail.

The phenomenon of high-hopes-soon-dashed has been well documented in research on the college presidency. With the average length of service for presidents being about seven years (Ross, Green, and Henderson, 1993), questions emerge about the lessons one should learn before assuming the leadership position. Finding ways to share the extraordinary burdens of the job enhances the chief officer's own capability and helps to develop future leaders. In fact, we should be placing less emphasis on the leadership of one or a few individuals and instead be thinking of how to create a culture of leadership that will empower all members of the institution.

NEW DIRECTIONS FOR HIGHER EDUCATION, no. 87, Fall 1994   © Jossey-Bass Publishers

A Learning Organization for Our Faculty and Staff

An institution characterized by a culture of leadership has features of the learning organization described by Peter Senge, a management consultant and faculty member in MIT's Sloan School of Management. According to Senge, the goal should be to build an organization where people from all levels are continually learning how to learn together. The key to that learning is a sense of connection between the individual's concerns and those of the greater whole. The real leaders of the organization are those who are not only open learners themselves but are also able to inspire in others the confidence and the will to work collectively in creating new answers as well as new issues. The people in a learning organization who emerge as leaders, therefore, are not necessarily those in positions of formal authority (Senge, 1990).

Benefits of a Leadership Culture

One benefit of a culture of leadership is a focus on institutional problem solving as opposed to strategies that primarily benefit individual interests. When members of the institution are provided with opportunities for developmental experiences, they are likely to have more positive perceptions of themselves in relation to the institution. In turn, broader knowledge of how they and their units fit into the big picture can help illuminate connections not before recognized. Sometimes those new awarenesses can lead to increased creativity and commitment for approaching large problems. In short, as personal considerations diminish in importance, thinking becomes institutional in character.

In an institution with a culture of leadership, individuals tend to be recognized less on the basis of status or position than on demonstrated potential. Dialogue occurs readily and information is generally accessible. People feel included, not excluded. In being recognized and affirmed for their contributions, individuals receive incentives for broader participation.

The results of inclusiveness are positive for the institution. One consequence is that larger talent pools are prepared for future personnel needs. Furthermore, talent is more readily available internally for providing relief in troubled times. Too often, in fact, institutions engage consultants who are less competent than the institution's own people. Too often, really fine professionals in college and university administration find that to be recognized for what they have to offer, they must relocate. Where there is a culture of leadership, the entire talent pool available to the institution is fully used.

An institutional focus on leadership possibilities for everyone has special meaning for minorities and women, who traditionally have not experienced equal participation in leadership positions. By providing opportunities for minorities and women to develop new skills, take part in activities beyond their normal spheres, develop networks, observe role models, and learn effective ways to communicate their views, an institution can establish for itself a prime pool of candidates for senior positions as they come open. Such availability can greatly enhance goals of affirmative action and increase the likelihood for meaningful diversity. In fact, success in this area tends to breed success. By promoting and making visible development opportunities for the traditionally underrepresented groups, an institution will eventually attract an even richer pool of talent for its position openings as others recognize that the institution pays more than lip service to the goals of affirmative action.

Need for a Culture of Leadership

Despite the obvious benefits of a leadership culture, higher education has been slow in recognizing its value. Robert Shoenberg of the Association of American Colleges has pointed out that such lack of attention to leadership development has serious consequences for colleges and universities (Shoenberg, 1993). Authority for decision making in academia is generally diffused. Faculty, students, and even staff members have certain prerogatives, and leadership is thus exerted although it is ineffective or even misinformed. To provide the most benefit to the organization, those who have a voice in decision making should be assisted in recognizing relationships between individual and unit or group concerns and larger issues of the institution. By making that connection, they are more likely to serve as positive leaders.

Developing leaders for higher education requires investing in people. The American higher education community seems prepared to acknowledge the importance of developing its human resources, largely out of necessity. The many pressures on higher education, including society's expectations of more and different kinds of services, are accelerating while resources are diminishing. Everywhere, in fact, faculty and staff are required to do more with less. There is a growing demand for greater access for more students, for greater relevance of university programs to the world of work, for increased responsibility by universities in economic growth, for lowering or at least maintaining tuition levels, and for outcomes assessment.

Constrained by all these factors, many institutions have been diligently reexamining themselves. In the process of downsizing, restructuring, and reengineering, some university leaders have begun to ask how they can make better use of existing faculty and staff in responding to the accelerating demands of society.

Reevaluating Human Resources

Although personnel expenses are drastically important from a budgetary perspective (on most campuses, they represent 80 percent or more of the total operating budget), most institutions currently allocate very little for development of their human resources. When times get tough, programs for development of faculty and staff are especially vulnerable. There are signs, however, that colleges and universities are reevaluating the role of human resource development. Even, during the early 1990s, when times have been especially difficult for higher education, a number of leadership development programs have flourished; others have remained viable through extraordinary commitment and creativity of their directors and sponsors. Many of the programs described in subsequent chapters have been initiated or reinspired during a period of fiscal difficulty.

A clue to greater interest by senior administrators in supporting human resource enhancement and in leadership development programming is in the titles of workshops and presentations at their national conferences. For example, the 1994 National Conference of The American Association for Higher Education opened with an address on "Reimagining the 21st Century Academic Workplace" and featured programs on faculty job satisfaction, academic career ladders, organizational restructuring, leadership strategies for women, team building, and improving the status of part-time faculty. In 1993, the National Association for College and University Business Officers (NACUBO) sponsored a three-day conference entirely on the subject of leadership. Titled "Leadership for the 21st Century," the program was repeated in 1994 and promises to be a successful component of the NACUBO curriculum. Most recent presentations have focused on leadership and the quality improvement process, the role of the chief financial officer in assisting change, and teamwork as the key to effective leadership.

Finding better approaches to human resource management was the theme of an international conference held in 1993 in Williamsburg, Virginia. There, college and university presidents and rectors representing eighteen nations defined the task of transforming higher education as one of "renewing human resources." One of the challenges of that goal implies more involvement by faculty members and administrators other than presidents and rectors in tackling broad institutional issues.

Ways to Create a Culture of Leadership

A number of approaches are being used by colleges and universities to inspire new thinking about leadership by faculty and staff. Some of these involve extrinsic activities that, in turn, stimulate ongoing initiatives in the home environment. For example, some institutions sponsor attendance at off-campus programs such as the Institute for Educational Management and the Management Development Program of Harvard University Graduate School of Education; the Center for Creative Leadership; and the Higher Education Resource Services (HERS) Summer Institute for Women at Bryn Mawr. Such experiences can be especially productive for attendees as well as their colleagues in the sponsoring institution when follow-up activities at home incorporate the new insights into the job.

The establishment of internal programming is another strategy that represents a growing trend. Some of the internal programs, variously identified as academy, institute, and seminar series, are basically stand-alone media targeted for selected audiences and aimed at improving management skills, inspiring big-picture concepts, and broadening career opportunities. Others are an outgrowth of a comprehensive employee development program, sometimes identified as training and development or organization development. Such programs approach leadership development as an indirect but significant side effect of the process of helping university employees, usually staff, become more competent and confident in their jobs. Having played a vital role in building support for the idea of leadership development, some of these have been expanded to include specialized offerings for faculty and senior administrators.

The many excellent examples of leadership development programs in this volume indicate that universities are beginning to recognize the critical role their own faculties and staffs will play in helping to meet the challenges of the future. Those challenges will not be merely financial; they will relate to more clouded issues, such as the identity and purpose of higher education in a technological society, the survival of autonomy amid increasing regulation, and the question of higher education as a fundamental right. Such issues are indeed daunting. Higher education cannot afford to rest its future in the hands and the heads of only a few good people. Creating a culture of leadership is a way of sharing both the responsibilities and the opportunities of future challenges and will go far in ensuring that higher education will have the human resources needed for shaping its own destiny amid inevitable demands for change.

References

Ross, M., Green, M. F., and Henderson, C. *The American College President: A 1993 Edition.* Washington, D.C.: Center for Leadership Development, American Council on Education, 1993.

Senge, P. M. *The Fifth Discipline: The Art and Practice of the Learning Organization.* New York: Doubleday, 1990.

Shoenberg, R. E. "Developing Informed, Effective Campus Leaders." *Chronicle of Higher Education,* Sept. 1, 1993, p. A68.

PHYLLIS H. LEWIS is director of human resources at the University of Pennsylvania.

Internships provide new, challenging temporary positions from which employees can gain new insights, skills, and perspectives related to their jobs and to leadership.

Institution-Sponsored Internships

Anne K. Ard

Unique opportunities to grow and enrich our professional lives are often precious and few. When that window of opportunity opens, a person must decide quickly whether to pass through or forever wonder what could have been. For me, deciding to apply for the Administrative Fellowship was such a moment. By deciding to compete I made a personal commitment to expand my horizons and to look for new challenges. The experience of the fellowship provided precious time to study and learn, to observe and collaborate, and to question and define dimensions of higher education in general and Penn State in particular. It was, for me, a very good year!
—Nancy Herron, Penn State Administrative Fellow, 1990–1991
(Pennsylvania State University, 1993)

Contrary to popular wisdom, leaders are made, not born. Many institutions of higher education have recognized in recent years that leadership potential in individuals must be nurtured and nourished. If leadership is, as Bensimon and Neumann (1993) contend, a "shared, interactive, culturally framed activity" (pp. xi–xii), then potential leaders in colleges and universities must have the opportunity to learn the culture and interact with those currently in leadership positions. Institutionally sponsored fellowships and internships, in-house opportunities to participate in the day-to-day activities of leadership, can provide such opportunities in a unique way. This chapter examines several administrative fellowships and internships that are currently operating or have recently ceased. A comparison of the programs will highlight the advantages and disadvantages of institution-sponsored programs and provide insights into the components necessary for a successful program. (See also the discussion

NEW DIRECTIONS FOR HIGHER EDUCATION, no. 87, Fall 1994   © Jossey-Bass Publishers

about the Association of California Community College Administrators Mentor Program in Chapter Five.)

Penn State Administrative Fellows Program

Of the several programs reviewed for this chapter, the only institution-sponsored fellowship that continues to function is the Administrative Fellows Program at Pennsylvania State University. Proposed by Penn State's Commission for Women in 1986, the program was accepted by university president Bryce Jordan and begun in 1986–1987 with one administrative fellow working in the office of the senior vice president for finance and operations. Originally designed to provide administrative mentoring for women, the program was expanded in 1989 to include men of racial and ethnic minorities.

The objectives of the Administrative Fellows Program are to identify women and minorities who have shown potential for effective leadership; increase awareness of the complex issues facing higher education; enhance understanding of the environment in which decisions are made; provide opportunities for participation in a wide range of decision-making processes, learning activities, and program management; and increase the pool of qualified women and minorities interested in higher-level administrative positions both inside and outside the Penn State community.

The program offers three full-time placements for women and racial and ethnic minorities in the senior administration of the university. Each fellow works with a mentor, either the executive vice president and provost, the senior vice president and dean of the seventeen-campus commonwealth education system, or with both the vice president for finance and the vice president for business and operations.

Logistical support for the program, including the call for applications and the application and selection process, is located in the Office of Human Resources. The application process is competitive and rigorous, involving an extensive application essay and a series of interviews. Approximately forty people apply each year for the three positions. The program is not limited to those in specific faculty or staff ranks, but the criteria for selection include "demonstrated success in their current positions and interest in administrative careers" and "evidence of leadership experience and decision-making ability" (Pennsylvania State University, 1993).

Because the fellowships are full-time and for an academic year, the home unit of each fellow receives compensation in order to replace the fellow for the year. These funds are provided from central administrative budgets. Fellows receive their normal salary during the fellowship year.

Each administrative fellow is expected to develop a learning plan for the year in consultation with her or his mentor. "The objective of the learning plan is the integration of theoretical knowledge and practical skills needed to provide a solid basis for participation in various problem-solving and decision-making projects" (Pennsylvania State University, 1994). Learning plans vary in the level of formality; however, it is expected that each fellow will come to the program with an idea of the types of activities in which she or he would like to be involved. Past fellows have participated in budget presentations, child care planning, university strategic planning, and minority student retention programs, for example.

By a variety of criteria, the Administrative Fellows Program at Penn State has been successful. Of the fifteen former fellows, ten have moved into new jobs with increased administrative responsibilities, although participation in the fellows program does not guarantee an administrative appointment. Of those who have moved into administrative positions, three have relocated to other colleges or universities. Former fellows speak glowingly of their fellowship year and perceive it to have been an extremely useful experience: "The Fellowship gave me a greater understanding and appreciation of how the decision-making and implementation processes within our administrative system work. It also provided me with significant opportunities to enhance my professional profile through actively participating in the process and recommending refinements to the system. Even more important were the significant relationships established with some of the very best people that Penn State has to offer" (Lydia Abdullah, administrative fellow, 1989–1990, in Pennsylvania State University, 1993). Fellows typically maintain close contact with their mentors and with each other, meeting regularly with other former fellows.

Despite increasingly severe financial constraints, as well as a change in the university's leadership, the Administrative Fellows Program has flourished at Penn State. It has done so, in part, because of continued advocacy by the Commission for Women, visible and vocal support of former fellows, and a commitment by Penn State administrators to increase the internal pool of women and racial and ethnic minorities qualified for administrative leadership.

Programs for Professional Enrichment at Eastern Illinois University

Like the Penn State program, the Programs for Professional Enrichment were conceived as an institutional response to the lack of women and racial and ethnic minorities in university administration. The Programs for Professional Enrichment were begun as a way to increase the numbers of women and racial and ethnic minorities by offering exposure to and mentoring within central administrative structures (Anderson, 1986).

Although administered through the Affirmative Action Office, once the programs began, they were open to all employees, regardless of race, gender, professional classification, or faculty rank.

The program at Eastern Illinois had three phases, each building on the one before it. Phase One, the Career Development Phase, was a fifteen- to twenty-hour program of workshops aimed at career planning. Workshops included career self-assessment, review and analysis of career options in higher education, and career advancement strategies. Employees applied for the program and were accepted into Phase One by a coordinating committee. In this phase, participants numbered about twenty each year (Anderson, 1986).

Phase Two, the Seminars in Higher Education Administration Phase, was open to any participant who had successfully completed the Career Development Phase. The seminars were held throughout the semester and were conducted by administrators from Eastern Illinois University, the Board of Governors of Illinois State Colleges and Universities, and administrators from other institutions of higher education. Topics included trends in higher education, leadership issues, financial management, and organizational development (Anderson, 1986).

The final phase of the programs was the Administrative Internship Phase. Participants in the first two phases of the programs were invited to submit proposals for administrative internships. The proposals were reviewed by the coordinating committee and internships were awarded to four people in the first year of the programs. The internships were part-time for one semester and interns normally received paid time off from their other university jobs for their participation. The Eastern Illinois Professional Enrichment Programs and the Affirmative Action Office hope to resume the internships in the near future (Judith Anderson, personal correspondence, 1994).

Management Internships Program
at Arizona State University

As part of a larger Management Development Program at Arizona State University (described elsewhere in this volume), the Management Internship was designed like its counterparts at Penn State and Eastern Illinois to provide women and racial and ethnic minorities opportunities for intensive exposure to university administration. Like the Eastern Illinois Programs, the Management Internship at ASU was open to any full-time staff, administrators, or faculty, not just women and racial and ethnic minorities (Arizona State University, 1993).

The Management Internship Program had several goals, including providing a pool of potential managers to ASU, supporting a program of promotional succession, disseminating ASU policies and philosophy, offering development opportunities to women and racial and ethnic minorities, and helping participants achieve their career goals in higher education administration (Arizona State University, 1993).

Seven interns were selected annually on a competitive basis to work with the president and each vice president. Interns were actively involved in the work of the offices to which they were assigned, serving as administrative staff support to the president or vice president with whom they worked. Although specific responsibilities were negotiated between the intern and his or her mentor, general responsibilities included research and analytical work, design and implementation of new programs, serving on committees as a representative of the mentor, and assisting in budget preparation (Arizona State University, 1993).

Similar to the Penn State Fellows Program, the Management Internship at ASU was full-time, lasting for nine months. The interns received their normal salaries and the units from which they came received compensation to replace them while they were serving as interns.

Unfortunately, the Management Internship Program was discontinued as part of the overall Management Development Program at ASU. Although limited opportunities still exist, budgetary constraints and a shift in institutional management philosophies caused the internship to be discontinued (Susan L. Courtney, personal correspondence, 1993).

Advantages and Disadvantages of Institution-Sponsored Programs

Given the proliferation of institution-sponsored internships in the 1980s and the demise of many of those same programs in the 1990s, a critical review of their advantages and disadvantages is crucial. On the positive side, administrative fellowships and internships provide an opportunity for women and racial and ethnic minorities to receive the mentoring necessary for understanding the administrative culture in higher education. The intense involvement in the day-to-day events of central administration provides experience simply unavailable through other means. The mentoring relationship may last long past the fellowship or internship, providing needed contacts as the intern continues on his or her professional path.

Although it is possible to limit the internships to women and racial and ethnic minorities, many institutions chose not to do so. Limiting eligibility for the program guarantees that historically underrepresented groups benefit, but it can cause distress within majority populations. Institutions must make conscious choices about this issue before moving ahead with internships.

Several people involved in the administration of fellowships or internships raised the issue of the need to leave an institution in order to advance professionally. Common wisdom seems to hold that in order to move into the most senior executive ranks in higher education administration, one must move to a different institution. Accordingly, experiences in an internship that are readily generalizable may be particularly helpful.

Clearly, the primary disadvantage of institution-sponsored fellowships and internships is the cost. Interns continue to receive at least their normal salary, and replacements in the home unit must be provided during the fellowship year. Additional costs may include support staff, additional seminars, travel, and facilities. In times of fiscal austerity, many institutions may not feel the cost is justified. Clearly, financial considerations played major roles in the demise of the program at Eastern Illinois and Arizona State Universities.

Fellowship and internship programs are the most comprehensive commitment higher education institutions can make to the leadership development of faculty and staff. The benefits to the university are clear—increased diversity in the administrative ranks and a stronger, more experienced pool of candidates for executive responsibilities. Though expensive to maintain, such programs may prove to be an efficient means to a more effective university administration.

References

Anderson, J. "Programs for Professional Enrichment, Eastern Illinois University." Paper presented at the College and University Personnel Association National Conference, Oct. 14, 1986.

Arizona State University. "The Management Development Program." Tempe: Arizona State University, 1993. Information packet.

Bensimon, E. M., and Neumann, A. *Redesigning Collegiate Leadership: Teams and Teamwork in Higher Education.* Baltimore: Johns Hopkins University Press, 1993.

Pennsylvania State University. "The Administrative Fellows Program for Women and Minorities Brochure," University Park: Pennsylvania State University, 1993.

Pennsylvania State University. "The Administrative Fellows Program for Women and Minorities Brochure," University Park: Pennsylvania State University, 1994.

ANNE K. ARD is senior diversity planning analyst for the Pennsylvania State University.

Increasingly, presidents must develop both as leaders and as part of leadership teams; such development requires conscientious planning and follow-up.

Developing Institutional Teams

James P. Gallagher

> The major test of a modern American University is how wisely and
> how quickly it adjusts to important new possibilities.
> —Clark Kerr (quoted in Keller, 1983, p. 40)

One night in 1945, General Dwight Eisenhower walked along the Rhine, thinking of the crossing in which he would lead the allied armies the following day. He met a soldier along the way and asked him why he was not sleeping.

The young G.I., who did not recognize the Supreme Allied Commander, said, "I guess I'm a little nervous."

"Well, so am I," Eisenhower responded. "Let's walk together by the river and perhaps we'll draw strength from each other" (Reiner, 1988).

Colleges and universities can learn a valuable lesson from this example. Just as General Eisenhower recognized that he and the young soldier could work together for their common good, higher education institutions can draw strength in these challenging times by pulling together and using their vast human resources at every level.

Doing so is a must in these troubled times. In 1983, George Keller sounded an alarm that the nation's 3,100 colleges and universities were living through a revolution, causing "unprecedented dismay, confusion, and handwringing" (1983, p. viii). The problems that led Keller to that conclusion have only worsened. There is increased competition for fewer high school graduates, increased demand for financial aid, and declining federal and state

---

All team development descriptions and quotations in this chapter are based on personal communication with the author.

New Directions for Higher Education, no. 87, Fall 1994 © Jossey-Bass Publishers

support. Such factors have turned this revolution into academic hand-to-hand combat.

Money, obviously, is the biggest problem. To stay afloat, colleges and universities are fighting over the same shrinking federal and state dollars while trying to keep tuition down and attract the best students. In a survey called "Campus Trends," the American Council on Education noted that 57 percent of all colleges and universities saw their operating budgets cut in 1991–1992, an increase of 12 percent over the previous year (De Witt, 1992).

Academics are aware of the current situation, but too many of them believe that higher education's current fiscal woes, however serious, are temporary. They think the solution is to just do some judicious belt tightening until the money starts pouring in once again from government coffers. At Philadelphia College of Textiles and Science (PCT&S), however, we concur with Robert Atwell, president of the American Council on Education, that "things will not get better until some time after the year 2010" (Elfin, 1992, p. 100). Therefore, we are relying on sound management techniques to control our destiny.

There is at least some truth in the saying that a college president is often defined as a person who lives in a big house and begs. One should add that a president, like a good coach or parent, must be a prophet, cheerleader, psychologist, and chief executive officer. To succeed at any of these duties, presidents must build a management team of superior people and do whatever is necessary to set the stage for a positive work environment.

An important first step is to assess the institution's strengths and weaknesses. Is there a long-range plan in place to serve as a beacon? Are key administrators creative and productive? Are new faculty and administrative positions needed? Is the college attracting high-quality students? Are the physical plant facilities adequate? Are faculty and staff pulling together for the common good? Where should the institution be five years from now? In ten years?

The list of questions that must be answered in any assessment is almost endless. Answers become apparent, however, when one seeks input from a large number of campus constituents, especially trustees, faculty members, administrators, alumni, and students; focuses on the important issues of challenges first; calls on outside consultants and colleagues from other institutions for their advice; and takes adequate time for the assessment amid what at times seems to be constant interruptions.

Presidents also must be aware that, when faced with problems and pressures, there is a tendency for some faculty members and administrators to become extremely anxious. The root cause of their anxiety, naturally enough, is concern over funding for their programs or projects. Campus leaders, once aware of this phenomenon, must take steps to make certain that self-preservation does not lead to destructive behavior by undermining the unity of the institution.

To keep this from happening, the president must work hard at creating a work environment in which administrators, faculty members, trustees, students and other campus constituents can work together constructively to solve problems. Effective policy making, as Wildavsky (1979) has noted, is one-third data and two-thirds interaction.

Interaction was important to Peter Burnham when he took over as president of Brookdale Community College in 1991. He initiated a mission-driven, team-building exercise that lasted four months. At three retreats for trustees, topics discussed included theory of leadership at community colleges, how they operate, their organizational structure, and their missions. "The process brought our own mission into focus, along with ideas of how to fulfill it," said Burnham (personal communication).

Meetings were then held for Burnham's senior staff. "This part of the process," said Burnham, "helped members of our campus leadership team to understand what their niche was—how they fit into the implementation of the mission.

"From that kind of team building began to flow institutional goals and objectives that reflected an integrated, strategic approach, as opposed to the old system under which everyone did his or her own thing.

"As a result of this approach, we began to understand the incredibly important interrelationships among the organizational units of the college, as well as the individuals who headed them up" (personal communication).

Burnham wisely encouraged his trustees and senior officers to engage in an open exchange of ideas and opinions. Where there is much desire to learn, wrote John Milton in his *Areopagitica* in 1644, "there, of necessity, will be much argument, much writing, many opinions; for opinion in good men is but knowledge in the making" (p. 406).

Shirley Chater, now commissioner of the Social Security Administration, recognized the importance of eliciting opinions from team members when she served as president of Texas Woman's University. She encouraged staff and faculty "to be open to new ideas, to be willing to be vulnerable and to take risks. An administrator can go along with the status quo, or, take a risk and make a difference" (Martin, 1989, p. E16). To her, creativity is infectious, and faculty members active in decision making are exemplary role models for students who will, in turn, affect others positively when they go out into the world.

Openness, too, is the electricity that energizes members of the President's Council at PCT&S. Each of the eight members knows that he or she has a mandate to say or do whatever necessary to make the campus more responsive to its students. They are, in effect, like musicians in a symphony orchestra. Each plays a certain instrument well, but, for the sake of harmony, reads from the same score.

These musicians are not robots plugged into integrated circuits. The academic vice president, the treasurer, the vice president of student affairs, and other members of the President's Council are individualists interested in team building. Of particular help to me is a staff member who comes into my office and says, "Listen, Jim. We just had a meeting and the project being proposed would be a disaster," or, "We've been working on this project for four months and we're wasting time. Nothing is happening." Such objectivity helps me sharpen my decisions.

Without objective input, our long-range plan would not have evolved into an effective guide to the future. Discussions, for example, led us to the belief that money—not historical mission—should be the driving force in the planning process. All too many college presidents and their faculty place too much emphasis on historical mission based on years of tradition. It is a mistake to do so.

The mission of colleges, buffeted by such forces as retrenchment, new technology, unfavorable demographics, and cultural diversity, is changing radically. Focusing faithfully on its historical past could result in "mission madness" or the tendency to adhere to wishful thinking. Pursuit of an outdated mission can seriously inhibit a college's ability to adapt to change and properly serve its students.

In developing our long-range plan, for example, we took a close, hard look at what funds would be available for the next three to six years. We sought new ideas from all campus constituents that challenged the status quo, but were realistic enough not to put the college's future at risk. It was therefore important to base our discussions and recommendations on trust and solid facts. We also took great pains to ensure that no one was left out.

The result was a series of three-year plans that will take PCT&S to the year 2000. The master plan recommends physical plant improvements and projects for creating a campus environment that enhances the quality of student life. Included is a realistic financial target for the college to fund.

Trust Is a Must

Without an environment of trust on campus, no leadership can be effective. Clearly, someone who is liked and trusted by others is most able to exert influence over them (Tedeschi, Lindskold, Horai, and Gahagan, 1969).

The key to developing a trusting environment, as Gardner points out (1986, p. 19) is "fairness—fairness when the issues are being openly adjudicated but, equally important, fairness in the backroom. . . . Nothing is more surely stabilizing than confidence that the leader is unshakably fair in public and in private."

To earn the trust and confidence of campus constituents, presidents also should follow these guidelines:

Listen more, talk less. Bad listening can lead to a breakdown in the decision-making process.
Nurture a good working relationship with trustees, whose support makes progress possible.
Follow the three F's of good management: be fair, friendly, and firm.
Be willing to admit mistakes.

Delegate responsibility.

Give people more credit than they deserve.

Show enthusiasm for other people's ideas as well as your own.

Have a sense of humor. Even during the darkest days of the Civil War, Abraham Lincoln eased tensions by telling a joke or humorous story.

Be willing to compromise. Presidents who get their way too often probably aren't doing a very good job.

Develop an Effective Hiring Process

Building a good management team starts with the selection process. The objective of any search should be to come up with a list of candidates that contains at least one superstar.

In our personnel searches at PCT&S, we look closely at the educational and professional backgrounds of candidates. Once those are reviewed, however, we focus our attention on fit, or the attributes required for a person to be a creative and productive member of the management team. Personnel consultant Richard Irish refers to such qualities as "flair factors" or "that vital talent, skill, capacity, orientation or ineffable intangible without which no candidate—no matter how well recommended or otherwise qualified—can succeed on the job" (Irish, 1975, p. 71). If an academic dean cannot develop relevant curriculum changes, for example, all of his or her educational credits are useless.

All of our team members, however, must have two flair factors in common: energy and enthusiasm. Pursuing a dream or vision as a campus leader requires endless energy, much enthusiasm, and persistent dedication to the pursuit of goals. We seek track stars, not sumo wrestlers, and people who get excited about the spirit of the chase.

We seek to identify those qualities through a close check of references, listed and unlisted, and a series of pertinent questions: What do you think of our work environment? What contributions would you make toward attaining the college's goals? Tell us about your three top achievements in your last position. What does it take to be productive in your line of work? We also look for signs of ambition in candidates—an assistant dean of admissions who wants to be the dean, or an academic dean who aspires to fill the president's shoes.

Communicate Expectations

Once staff are hired, it is important for a president and other administrators to do the following:

Let them know from the start what is expected of them.

Give them clear directions. People do not follow leaders who lack a compass.

Delegate responsibilities to those who can handle them well. No leader ever accomplishes anything alone.

Always give credit. Giving public credit to someone who has earned it is the
best leadership technique.
Help them to develop their careers.
Encourage them to suggest and initiate new ideas.
Provide them with constant support.
Devote money and time to their professional development.
Create an environment of celebration. When people get excited about
their work, they pour a lot of energy into it. Enthusiasm is certainly con-
tagious.
Dream along with them.

Foster Professional Development

Most people, according to management experts, work at about 60 percent of
their capacity. We attempt to raise this level at PCT&S. For example, at staff
meetings, I tell my top officers, "It's my job to push you to the extreme limit
without being a Simon Legree." However, I have to be wise enough to say,
"Okay. We've gone far enough, and you have to be smart enough to tell me that
the workload is getting to be too much. Then I'll back off." We try to set a high
work standard for the entire campus. Without being unethical about it, we ask
everyone to do more with less.

To help managers reach their potential, we make their professional development a top priority. Adequate funds are budgeted yearly for this purpose.
Members of the President's Council, for example, are encouraged to attend
Harvard's Institute for Educational Management (IEM). Each officer also is
given a sabbatical every seven years to get some well-earned rest and recre-
ation, which helps to keep them productive members of the administrative
team; enter an environment where they can learn something new or polish up
on their skills; and write a document, as an option, for publication or for sharing in-house with their colleagues.

Recently, for example, treasurer Tom Kingston spent a sabbatical studying
the programs and management styles of administrators at the University of
Brighton, a school in England that is much like PCT&S. "We learned much
from each other," he said.

Every six months, all council members also visit other campuses, such as
the Fashion Institute of Technology, Rhode Island School of Design, Carnegie-
Mellon University, and Duke University, to share ideas with their administrators. We reciprocate and act as hosts for other institutions. Recently, the top
administrators from Bowie State University came to PCT&S and our academic
dean met with their academic dean, our dean of admissions met with theirs,
and so forth. Reciprocal ventures such as these offer tremendous potential for
the exchange of ideas and personnel development.

In addition, every six months trustees, top officers, and some faculty members attend off-campus retreats to discuss the college's future. We regularly

invite outside experts on such subjects as academics, planning, finances, and architecture to join the discussions. These consultants serve as physicians who, through their examinations and advice, make certain that we are not doing anything foolish to undermine the health of our college.

We also encourage our middle managers, such as the directors of financial aid, placement, and security, to attend professional development seminars throughout the United States. Also under consideration are minisabbaticals for middle managers every seven years.

Many other colleges and universities are finding that it pays to send key members of the management team and some faculty to IEM and similar institutes. Harry Smith, president of Austin College, for example, regularly sends members of his executive cabinet to IEM with good results. "The case study method used there has been very useful to us," he said in an interview. "The shared experiences have helped our staff members become aware of issues outside of their own areas of expertise. As a result, they have learned to better analyze campus-wide problems, and to work together as a team in solving them."

Janet Greenwood, president of Longwood College from 1981 to 1987, credits IEM for helping her to turn around a school rumored to be either closed or merged with another public institution. "Senior staff members sent there developed a better understanding of what works at other institutions and whom to call to get things done," she said in an interview. "They also came out of the program with a shared vision." Greenwood also hired an outside consultant to conduct a study of opportunities, which was instrumental in helping her to reorganize her top staff.

North Carolina State University regularly sends up to twenty-four people to attend programs of the Center for Creative Leadership in Greensboro, North Carolina. Robert Clark, professor of business management and economics, initiated the effort as a means of seeking ideas for the development of the curriculum in leadership education. Administrators from other areas of the university also decided to participate to help the university to work better. The center also has held its special Looking Glass program on the NC State campus for twenty administrators. Featured on the program was a management simulation experience in running a glass company.

All of the programs, said Clark, were a useful experience in curriculum development, developing a team atmosphere and enhancing individual skills. "The programs have helped to improve interaction within our own and other colleges on campus," he said.

Develop Leadership

Colleges and universities can learn much from the corporate world about team building, said James Lyons, president of Jackson State University. "Higher education assumes things will come together automatically," he added. "Appoint faculty members to deans and deans to vice presidents and everyone will fall into step. My experience has shown me that this is not so."

While he was president of Bowie State University, Lyons noted, "we accepted the fact early on that teams were made, not born." Working with an outside management consultant, he had the Myers–Briggs Inventory Test given to campus administrators. "It was a fairly good indicator of one's personality, interests and style," said Lyons.

"The test pinpointed specific things about team members and how they were expected to respond to certain challenges. We learned, for example, who our aggressive administrators were and who were the caring and sensitive ones. Such information gave me some idea on how team members would operate in different situations."

According to Lyons, test results helped team members to become better managers and to gain insights into how their colleagues might respond to certain issues.

When he was president of Dakota Wesleyan University, James Beddow took his leadership off campus for development sessions. He chaired a strategic planning process, called Vision 2000, for the Mitchell, South Dakota, region. Four of his senior officers served on the task force along with various community leaders.

"Being a small university in a region with a declining population, we felt that we should do what we could to improve its viability and vitality," said Beddow. "Our work led to the development of the plan, a youth leadership minor in our curriculum, and strong leadership programs for county commissioners, city council and school board members, and other community leaders. We think that it is the new frontier for campus leadership. The task force also gave our campus officers an opportunity to work with diverse groups and gain experience in defining their own skills in organizing work, planning, and problem solving."

From Richard P. Traina, president of Clark University, comes an example of how to overcome what he calls contentious gridlock on campus. The faculty and administration, in effect, were unable to work together constructively.

At the time, Traina was devoting an extraordinary amount of time to a capital campaign, kicked off in 1987, and building better relations with Worcester and surrounding communities. Meanwhile, faculty relationships with the academic administrators were disintegrating over what course of action had to be taken in dealing with campus issues.

To break the gridlock, Traina initiated an administrative review by a team of external consultants from other universities and, internally, an evaluation by faculty members. The administrative review report, which took a year to prepare, was shared first with trustees, then with the entire campus community.

During the year-long study, Traina received good advice from a core group of faculty leaders who were "university-conscious people," the trustee leadership, and individual members of the external review team. Significant changes were made in the personnel and organizational structure. Also, a new strategic and financial plan was developed around which, said Traina, the "University is now galvanized."

According to Traina, several leadership lessons were learned from this experience. When a president is very much dedicated to external relations, he or she must be absolutely certain that senior officers are good and work well together. He or she must also make certain that the right people are in the right place at the right time. Different skills are needed at different times. At Clark, a factor in also helping to break the gridlock was selecting people from inside the school who were highly respected by their colleagues.

Traina noted that there is now a "tremendous spirit of cooperation on campus. This can be attributed primarily to the confidence the trustees showed in the university and the ability of the faculty to galvanize around the new academic administration." This bodes well for the future of Clark University.

Conclusion

As times change, colleges and universities must also learn to adapt to their environment. New and creative forms of leadership and management are required in order for institutions to turn potential problems into opportunities and to remain healthy. From the many examples I have noted, it is obvious that the key to success, and passing the major test to which Clark Kerr refers, lies in recognizing, developing, and using available personnel resources—faculty, administration, students, alumni, and trustees. By taking advantage of this large pool of talent, institutions can take a comprehensive approach to problem solving and planning.

References

De Witt, K. "Colleges Seeing More Students but Less Money." *New York Times,* Aug. 5, 1992, p. 88.

Elfin, M. "What Must Be Done." *U.S. News & World Report,* 1992, *113* (12), 100.

Gardner, J. W. *The Heart of the Matter: Leader-Constituent Interaction.* Leadership Papers 3. Washington, D.C.: INDEPENDENT SECTOR, 1986.

Irish, R. K. *If Things Don't Improve Soon I May Ask You to Fire Me: The Management Book for Everyone Who Works.* Garden City, N.Y.: Anchor Press, 1975.

Keller, G. *Academic Strategy: The Management Revolution in American Higher Education.* Baltimore: Johns Hopkins University Press, 1983.

Martin, D. "A Campus of Growth: Woman's University Offers Quality in an Atmosphere of Strong Support." *Austin American-Statesman,* Apr. 30, 1989, pp. E1, E16.

Milton, J. *Areopagitica.* In *Great Books of the Western World,* vol. 32. Encyclopedia Britannica, 1952.

Reiner, J. J. Speech delivered to the Omicron Delta Kappa. 75th Anniversary National Conference, Lexington, Ky., March 19, 1988.

Tedeschi, J. T., Lindskold, S., Horai, J., Jr., and Gahagan, J. P. "Social Power and the Credibility of Promises." *Journal of Personality and Social Psychology,* 1969, *13,* 253–261.

Wildavsky, A. *Speaking Truth to Power: The Art and Craft of Policy Analysis.* Boston: Little, Brown, 1979.

JAMES P. GALLAGHER is president of Philadelphia College of Textiles and Science.

Some institutions sponsor internal programs that demonstrate a commitment to developing new leaders among their own faculty and staff.

Campus-Based Academies, Institutes, and Seminar or Workshop Series

Phyllis H. Lewis, Laura M. Fino, Julie Y. Hungar, William H. Wallace, Jr., Richard F. Welch

A number of institutions have begun in-house programs for faculty and staff that firmly connect the leadership development concept with institutional goals. For example, some programs are designed to promote the institutional value of teamwork. Others demonstrate a special commitment to internal promotions and the career advancement of underrepresented groups in higher-level positions. All of them in one way or another aim to promote better institutional management, but some programs reflect this as a primary goal.

Usually these programs are very intensive. Some extend over a few weeks of nine-to-five-plus commitment. Others are set up as a series of seminar-type meetings once a month or once a week over an extended period. Follow-up activities providing ongoing opportunities for networking and exchange of ideas are scheduled in some cases.

The motivation and inspiration for these programs vary greatly. In some cases, the desire to provide better staff development for less money is a part of the rationale for expending institutional resources in this way. For example, far more individuals can participate in this type of internal program than can possibly attend, with institutional sponsorship, one of the expensive off-campus programs, such as the Harvard programs on educational management or the Higher Education Resource Services (HERS) Summer Institute for Women. However, the outcome of these programs is usually more keenly felt than would be possible from sending a smaller number of participants to an external program.

A number of institutions have set up programs that represent this model. Three of these—Arizona State University, Kennesaw State College, and the

Seattle Community College District—are described in terms of their creation, curricula and format, evaluation, participants, staffing, and funding. In addition to the three detailed profiles, notes concerning several other interesting programs are included at the end, with only unique features noted. A list of persons affiliated with the programs, with contact numbers, is provided in the Appendix.

Arizona State University's Leadership Academy

Laura M. Fino

In late 1986, Arizona State University (ASU) created an in-house management development program in order to meet the developmental needs of university administrators. The realization of the need for this program as well as its creation serves as a model of how an organization can critically assess itself and its processes and begin to change them.

The Management Development Program was largely the result of an examination of management hiring processes. The president was concerned that there were more outside hires for executives and managers of the university than promotions from within. After six months of investigation, promotions to middle- and senior-level positions did appear to be given to a large percentage of outside applicants. The reason most often given for this trend was that personnel at the university did not have the leadership training and skills needed in a higher-level position. Specifically, ASU's supervisory personnel lacked the ability to see and understand the big picture, to understand where the university was going, and to recognize how each of the colleges and departments contributed to that mission. The president felt that with leadership training, more of ASU's own people could qualify for these higher-level positions.

The president appointed a task force of faculty and administrators from each of the vice presidential areas and representatives from human resources, then charged this group with designing a training program for all university administrators. The president outlined seven steps to be addressed by the task force. As its beginning point, the task force defined a philosophy for the program: people are the most important resource—indeed, they are the key to the university's success.

The purpose of the program was expressed as the training and preparation of managers and supervisors, specifically to help them recognize and realize their full potential; to help them develop functional, interpersonal, and conceptual skills to use in their current assignments; to provide knowledge that will make them more effective in a variety of possible future assignments; and to prepare them to take on broader and more demanding assignments in the future.

Using ideas from focus groups, information from other organizations, and the expertise of its members, the task force set about designing a program. Its review of forty human resource development programs from business, government, and educational institutions revealed a paucity of management development materials devoted to the training of managers in a university setting. In designing a program, the task force was asked to consider the specific developmental needs of minorities and women.

The task force had originally intended to design a single training program for all those engaged in middle management activities across the university. However, focus groups strongly recommended a separate forum for academic chairs, who typically come into their positions without any training in management skills. Others in traditional management jobs usually have some basic knowledge of management skills through their experience at lower ranks. The final result was a proposal for a four-tiered management development program, one tier of which is the Leadership Academy.

The target audience of the academy is middle- and senior-level managers in academic and operational units. This includes job titles such as director, assistant and associate director, unit manager, and program coordinator. Although chairs and associate and assistant deans are encouraged to and do participate, other components of the management development program have been specifically designed to meet their needs.

Participation in each session of the Leadership Academy is limited to thirty-five people to allow meaningful class participation and to stay within budget constraints. Each vice presidential area is given a specific number of slots corresponding in ratio to the number of eligible people in that area. A nomination process, sponsored by the president's office, was put into place to emphasize the president's support of the program and to ensure that all those eligible have an equal opportunity to apply. As the academy has grown in reputation, the number of applications has grown as well.

The nomination process begins in July with the president issuing a request for nominations to the president's council. Applicants are usually nominated by their superiors. Selection of finalists is made within each vice presidential area on the basis of criteria unique to each area. Recommended guidelines include the individual's need to know the information provided in the Leadership Academy in order to perform the present or future job; the effect of time commitment; and the participation of women and minorities.

The focus and format of the academy has shifted a bit over the years, reflecting changes in higher education as well as attempts to respond to needs; however, the core objectives remain intact and continue to guide the program. These objectives are to communicate the management and leadership philosophy of ASU, to support and implement administrative initiative from upper management, to encourage communication among supervisors, and to support the development and implementation of the promotional management succession program at ASU.

In accomplishing the first two objectives, the Leadership Academy has become an increasingly important avenue of communication for upper administration. The president and the vice presidents share their philosophy and ideas with this select group; a dialogue then occurs that challenges the thinking of the participants and presenters. The last two objectives of networking and promotional succession have turned out to be the cornerstone of the academy. The opportunity to build collegial networks, establish new friendships, and have dialogue with senior administrators is reported in the year-end evaluation as the number-one benefit of academy participation. Through formal and informal relationships forged during the program, many participants have enjoyed visibility that has enhanced promotion opportunities.

The program format includes thirteen three-hour sessions extending from September through April. The academy's focus and curriculum emphasize leadership competencies rather than management skills. Current curriculum components include an overview of ASU's management philosophy, issues in higher education management (legal and personnel issues, media and public relations, leadership competencies, strategic planning, the budgeting process, diversity), 360 feedback instruments assessing management and leadership skills, and the legislative process.

The curriculum is flexible to allow coverage of timely issues and to reflect changing needs. For example, following an unprecedented reduction in state funding in 1990, participants began to receive intensive instruction on the importance of taking an active role in the political aspects of state funding for the institution. Recent sessions have focused on quality management in higher education, change and innovation in higher education, the campus as a community, valuing diversity, and principle-centered leadership. The training methods used have also evolved from the traditional approach of management training, with speakers presenting on a given topic and skill-building activities, to a more interactive and experiential approach.

The program's format is a result of several influences, one of which is the feedback gathered from academy participants. That feedback is considered an essential ingredient of the program and members are given ample opportunity to share their ideas. They are asked to complete a one-page evaluation after each session and an end-of-year evaluation. The session evaluation gives the program coordinator immediate feedback concerning a number of program issues. Participants are asked to rate the speakers on a numerical scale and to include a narrative response addressing the usefulness of the information on a personal and organizational level. A more in-depth evaluation, required two weeks after completion of the program, is intended to inspire reflections about the long-term value of the program.

Kennesaw State College's Leadership Programs for Faculty and Staff

William H. Wallace, Jr., Richard F. Welch

Kennesaw State College has instituted leadership development programs for faculty, staff, and students. These grew out of observations by president Betty

Siegel and others that enormous leadership potential within the faculty was not being fully used. There was no formal attempt to recognize and capitalize on this opportunity. The first effort, Leadership Kennesaw State College for faculty, was created in 1985 to develop this potential. It was designed to introduce faculty to new avenues of service and scholarship, to get them more directly involved with setting the goals and objectives of the college, and to create a dialogue between faculty and administration concerning the impact of organizational change. The concept was based on Leadership Georgia, a program of the Business Council of Georgia that recruits business and civic leaders for training and reflection. Initially, Leadership Kennesaw State College recruited senior faculty members with the aim that they would continue and expand their leadership roles on campus. It soon became apparent that junior faculty with leadership potential should also participate in the program.

In 1988, a second leadership program was created for staff employees. Staff Leadership Kennesaw State College was designed to develop and enhance leadership and team-building skills for classified staff employees, who make up more than 50 percent of the college employee population. The Staff Leadership program has a very basic premise: individuals who are expected and given the opportunity to assume roles of responsibility will do so; employees who perceive a sense of ownership in decisions that affect their work environment will have an increased sense of institutional commitment and loyalty.

Both programs have received national recognition. For example, the Staff Leadership program was selected by the College and University Personnel Association as one of the top five innovative human resource management projects implemented on college campuses for 1992–1993.

Membership in Leadership Kennesaw is open to tenure-track and tenured teaching faculty as well as administrative faculty members with at least one year of service. Staff Leadership is open to all classified employees, both hourly and professional or administrative. Each vice president's area is given a specific number of slots, corresponding in ratio to the number of eligible people in that area. Typically, a variety of employee groups (mechanics, laborers, secretaries, police, and so forth) are represented in a single class. Both programs limit participation to twenty to twenty-four members each year. College employees receive letters inviting them to apply or to nominate colleagues for program participation. Candidates are selected to ensure a diverse cross section of employees and faculty. Nominations generally exceed the number of available openings.

There are a number of similarities between the faculty and staff programs, but there are also some subtle differences. Both programs emphasize a team approach to solving institutional problems. They provide a forum for the exchange of ideas; identify internal and external opportunities for community involvement; explore institutional objectives as well as the political, economic, legal, and technological constraints on the institution; introduce specific leadership skills to enhance participants' effectiveness and efficiency; and create awareness and understanding of diversity.

At least once each year, participants from both leadership programs, together with members of Kennesaw State's Student Leadership program, come together to explore ways the three constituencies are linked. Some of the sessions have addressed skills and issues related to quality leadership and have explored opportunities for shared ventures.

Other common leadership program activities include an examination of the personal dimensions of leadership; issues of diversity and ethics in the workplace; the higher education governance structure, including meetings with state legislators and senior members of the University System of Georgia Board of Regents; and community outreach opportunities. Both programs require class members to participate in group projects that address either institutional or community problems. On the premise that a college, especially one such as Kennesaw State College, operates within a larger community, social issues are frequently addressed, such as inadequate or insufficient housing, hunger, and abuse of women and children; support groups for other disadvantaged groups constitute a civic and community responsibility.

The Leadership Kennesaw program for faculty has eight sessions during an academic year and Staff Leadership has six sessions, although the two programs do not run concurrently. To enhance the institution's commitment to teaching, Leadership Kennesaw addresses innovation in the classroom and the role of academics in the broader professional community of higher education. Staff Leadership supports staff employee career advancement opportunities by offering programs that create a knowledge base and leadership skills necessary for future administrative openings.

Both programs begin and end with off-campus retreats. The opening event helps to build a sense of group identity, teamwork, and unity away from daily interruptions. The final event provides an opportunity for closure, reflection, and overall program assessment.

Both programs have experienced changes over the years and will continue to change to meet the needs of the participants and the institution. Care has been taken to keep the programs fresh, but programming does not always keep pace with the needs of the participants. Leadership Kennesaw, for instance, is fortunate to include both academic and administrative (nonteaching) faculty. There is a tendency to concentrate more heavily on teaching in certain portions of the program, which leaves some administrative faculty disassociated. Staff Leadership faces that same challenge. Exempt and nonexempt employees have differing needs and interests.

Assessment is a major component of the leadership programs. Leadership Kennesaw has a steering committee made up of alumni who preview each month's program and suggest modifications based on their own experiences, the changing needs of the institution, and documented responses from previous leadership classes. Staff Leadership uses formal evaluation instruments completed by program participants at the conclusion of each respective session for assessment and modification purposes. In addition, the director of human resources relies on personal observations to incorporate program changes as new issues and needs arise.

The most meaningful assessment of these programs has been the measure of their worth to the institution. There is some impact on the individual because participation is regarded as a factor in faculty promotion considerations. However, the more significant institutional effects are greater cooperation between departments, a more complete understanding of the various academic disciplines and support departments, and lasting collegial relationships that spark personal and professional growth.

The degree to which these programs are integrated into the institution is apparent in the way they have helped change the culture. Several important institutional initiatives have their genesis in Leadership Kennesaw; these include the annual Philip C. Preston Community Service Award to recognize faculty community service contributions, the development of a handbook for part-time faculty, and a major conference to explore teaching and innovations in the classroom. Achievements of the Staff Leadership program include the creation of staff and middle-management supervisory training programs; development of the staff Employee of the Year Award; creation of a new employee orientation program; preparation of an office help manual for clerical and secretarial personnel; development of a comprehensive employee attitudinal survey assessing institutional strengths and weaknesses; and sponsorship of a road race, with proceeds used to support Disabled Student Services.

The costs of the respective programs are minimal in terms of overall institutional funding. The annual budget for Leadership Kennesaw is $5,500–$6,500 and the budget for Staff Leadership is approximately $1,000 less. Primary funding for the respective programs comes from the departmental budgets within which the programs are housed. Expenses incurred include two off-campus retreats, sweatshirts for program participants, books and other resource manuals for participants, certificates for successful program completion, and other miscellaneous expenses. Because state regulations prohibit use of state funds for food or beverages, additional funding for these items is provided through the Kennesaw State College Foundation.

Coordination of the programs is included as a part of the position responsibilities of the director of human resources (for the staff program) and the director of the Center for Excellence in Teaching and Learning (for the faculty program). No additional staff support is budgeted. Both directors rely on existing departmental staff to handle clerical support functions and logistical arrangements.

Members of the faculty and administration often serve as program presenters. This fosters a positive opportunity for faculty, administrators, and staff to work together. This effort facilitates an appreciation and respect among constituencies that is often neglected.

At the conclusion of this year, Leadership Kennesaw will have 225 alumni and Staff Leadership will have 150 alumni. Many of these colleagues have assumed leadership positions within the institution, and others have used this opportunity to advance professional and research activities with other classmates.

The programs will continue to undergo change and refinements to make them even more valuable. For example, former participants have noted something of a void after spending a year working closely and intensely. Requests have been made to create another level of leadership programming for alumni.

Leadership Academy of Seattle Community Colleges

Julie Y. Hungar

A key to developing a culture of cooperation and trust in a multicollege district is the forging of a unified and loyal team of administrators whose loyalty attaches to the district as well as to one's own college. One part of the strategy for building such a team in the Seattle Community Colleges is the Leadership Academy, a program initiated in 1993 by the district's chancellor, Charles A. Kane.

The Seattle colleges grew up in an environment that fostered divisiveness. That environment was characterized by rivalry among areas of the city for campus funding and programs, adversarial faculty–management relations, racial strife, and, perhaps most critical, lack of stability at the top. During its first twenty-five years, the district was led by a succession of nine chief executive officers and three interim chancellors. During one four-year period, the district was run by an executive committee of the three college presidents, each taking a turn as district president; this proved to be particularly successful in cementing the culture of competition.

In more recent times, the atmosphere had improved somewhat, but the divisions were still deep. When the Board of Trustees named Kane chancellor in 1992, they reemphasized their commitment to unity and their expectation that he would achieve it. He saw the molding of a cohesive management team as a priority. As one means of achieving that, he created the Leadership Academy.

The academy was adapted from a similar activity Kane had inaugurated during his fourteen-year tenure as president of Riverside Community College in California. Its purpose is threefold: to build a sense of common purpose and trust among administrators throughout the district, to ensure consistency in carrying out administrative policies and decisions, and to provide opportunity for professional development, which had been virtually nonexistent.

For the first academy, attendance was by invitation. About thirty-five district administrators from associate dean to president were included. The majority of those invited were instructional administrators. The focus of the program, teaching and learning, was selected to emphasize the district's first priority—direct service to students.

Subsequent sessions have included administrators from all areas and have had a broader focus. Participants spend four full days during the summer quarter in a team-building and professional development seminar with colleagues from across the district. They meet each day on a different campus; for some, this will be their first visit. The academy's fundamental objectives are to identify ways of serving students better through collaboration, coordination, and mutual support; to understand and commit to the district's values statement; to develop a common foundation of leadership theory; to acquire or expand specific management skills; to gain insight on current issues affecting the institution; and to develop working relationships with administrators across the district.

The academy program is built on several principles. First, it is intensive. Sessions begin at 7:30 A.M. and continue until 4:30 P.M., with working sessions over breakfast, a notebook of readings before the program, additional readings as homework, and presentations by participants and outside speakers. Second, it is interactive. Working groups are formed on the first morning and meet daily to carry out assigned projects; presenters are expected to involve the participants in their sessions. Third, it is substantive, covering topics that strike a balance between challenging big-picture subjects and practical, take-home information sessions. Not least important, fellowship and fun are established as values from the opening session.

Opportunities for administrators from across the district to get together and build a sense of teamwork have previously been limited, so project groups are deliberately structured to cross campus boundaries. The chancellor's intent to incorporate Academy members into a district team is quite explicit. Kane participates each day and presents at least one session, giving participants an opportunity to get to know him and to hear his views on management and where he sees the district heading. At the end of the program, he gives a summary presentation.

Sessions deal with such topics as effective leadership, team management, management styles, interest-based bargaining, the state budget model, time management, and faculty recruitment, selection, and evaluation. Thorny aspects of union bargaining agreements are explored. In a discussion of a controversial new workforce training law, the lobbyist who had opposed the colleges' position was part of a panel that included other members of the business community and government agency staff. Faculty members have been featured in sessions on values. Some topics vary depending on the makeup of the group; for example, topics for the first group addressed instructional interests and a subsequent program included topics of interest to student services and administrative services managers.

With an emphasis on active learning, the sessions demonstrate various delivery methods. These include lectures, panel discussions, small groups, fishbowls, practice work sessions, and group problem solving. A sample assignment is to develop and present a complete vision of what the district should look like in the year 2000. On the last afternoon of the academy, the work groups, who have been meeting daily to prepare their projects, report to the assembly.

Evaluation forms given out each day use a five-point rating scale and open-ended comments to evaluate each session. On the last day, participants are also asked to rate and comment on the total experience. An effort is made to collect the evaluations at the end of each day. From the first academy, this comment captures the flavor of the overall evaluations: "I came reluctantly— too much work, too much time away. I feel now that I would not have missed it for anything."

Beyond the strong ratings and positive comments, the results of the Leadership Academy for the Seattle Community Colleges have been increased collaboration among administrators around the district, new cooperation in program planning and grant proposals, a relaxing of tension, and an increase in good humor in district gatherings. An acid test of the spirit of cooperation engendered in the first academy came when Kane introduced another strategy the following fall. In a move that was quite revolutionary for the district, he asked the four chief instructional officers in the district—the vice chancellor for education and the campus vice presidents for instruction—to switch jobs with one another for an academic quarter. The exchange was accomplished with relatively little trauma, and it not only brought the four exchangees closer together as a team but also helped break down the barriers among all staff.

The academy is relatively inexpensive, except for participants' salary costs. Many presenters are themselves members of the team, and most outsiders have been pleased to donate their time. College facilities are used, so the major direct cost is for breakfast, lunch, and coffee breaks, and this comes from the chancellor's budget for development.

The benefits have justified costs in both time and money. The academy continues to influence the life of the institution as members from each year become an alumni group, holding their own alumni meetings and carrying forward cross-district dialogue begun during the academy. Some alumni apply for a second year; some recommend or direct others on their staff to attend.

Because it is sponsored by the chancellor and because it has effectively served its twofold purpose, the Leadership Academy will continue. Even after all district administrators have participated once, there will be a need to keep nurturing the team, to keep giving administrators opportunity for development. There will be new members to bring onto the team, new ideas for improving service to students. Extending a comparable opportunity to faculty, the district began a program modeled on the Great Teachers seminar in the year following the first Leadership Academy; the next evolution in Seattle could bring these two groups together to bridge the gulf between faculty and administrators.

University of Kentucky

The University of Kentucky (UK) has a new program, Effective Supervisory Principles (ESP), to develop the knowledge base and leadership abilities of supervisors. Paralleling the assessment center concept, the program is designed to be tailored for supervisors in a particular unit; for example, the pilot, which was delivered in early 1994, was directed to UK food service supervisors. In developing the program, the human resources staff led focus groups for compiling a list of attributes, qualities that may be helpful as one continues to develop and expand management skills. For example, attributes for the food service supervisors include the following: ensures product and service quality, communicates effectively, and manages stress.

During Phase 1 of ESP, supervisors of a homogeneous group receive three days of intensive training that covers a variety of topics: university mission, legal issues and personnel policies, principles of effective leadership, diversity, harassment, and performance appraisals. In addition, participants learn about the attributes for their group and prepare for their attribute assessment interview.

During Phase 2, each participant meets with his or her coach, who is also the participant's supervisor. That meeting focuses on how the participant measures up to the attribute profile. Both participant and coach are assisted in this process and during follow-up by a third-party advisor. The advisor is someone outside the work unit but within the UK community who has been identified as having strong supervisory skills. The participant sets quarterly goals for working toward improvement on the attribute profile. All three persons—participant, coach, and advisor—work together in a structured way over a two-year period. A recognition ceremony at the end of Phase II provides formal closure to the process.

University of Nebraska–Lincoln Institute of Agriculture and Natural Resources

The Office of Professional and Organizational Development sponsors a number of developmental programs for faculty and administrators. One of these is the University of Nebraska Professional Renewal of Faculty (NUPROF), which has served more than a hundred faculty from UNL and other institutions. In NUPROF, participants are encouraged to recognize the role change plays in their professional and personal lives and to learn how to manage change for their own and their institution's advantage. Program activities begin with the Faculty Development Institute, a three-day off-campus retreat. After the institute, participants are encouraged to assess strengths and needs and to explore other opportunities for development, using colleagues and others as resources. Participants work independently, in small groups, or in interinstitutional teams. The culmination of the exploring phase is the individual professional development plan, which may be carried out with some funding from the institution. Some examples of projects that have been a part of growth plans are as follows: pursue education in creative problem solving; decide on career directions, professional development, and the opportunity to work on a student-oriented service; and develop expertise in international education. After a year or two, participants evaluate the achievement of their growth plans.

Western Kentucky University

Western Kentucky University's program, called Leadership for the '90s, was initiated in 1993 by president Thomas Meredith to provide an active process for organizational renewal. Currently, the program operates from the department of continuing education. Participation is required for all WKU administrators and managers who evaluate staff. Groups of thirty participants cycle through the seminars over eighteen months, with multiple groups working at the same time. Classes are made up of persons from different areas of the university who occupy widely varying roles. For example, a physical plant supervisor may work with a faculty supervisor. Topics cover four major areas: management development, human relations, personal development, and issues and policies. Presenters are WKU faculty and administrators as well as others with special expertise from outside the university.

One motivation for the program is to provide a cost-effective way to facilitate staff development. As conceived originally, it is designed to serve as a prerequisite for selection to participate in significant off-campus professional development experiences. Current plans are to arrange follow-up activities for alumni of the program in the form of group projects. Eventually, the program may be broadened to include staff.

University of North Carolina at Chapel Hill

The UNC-CH program, called BRIDGES, is a professional development program for women in academia who seek to acquire and refine leadership capabilities. It was developed in 1993 following requests for such a program from UNC-CH's Coalition for Women's Concerns. Participants have the opportunity to gain knowledge about university administration and its challenges as well as a chance to build networks and mentoring relationships. The program also focuses on self-understanding and emphasizes achieving balance in one's personal and professional life.

There are four parts to the program—leadership, academic institutions, skill building, and preparing for the future. Presenters include members of the university community and guest speakers. The program begins with a weekend session, with most sessions occurring on a weeknight or during a weekend day.

The program is guided by an advisory board and managed by UNC-CH's Division of Continuing Education. Participants are selected on the basis of applications and recommendations. Some slots are open for participants from other campuses within the University of North Carolina system. Fees are set at around $1,200, with some scholarship assistance being available from the various participating campuses.

PHYLLIS H. LEWIS is director of human resources at the University of Pennsylvania.

LAURA M. FINO is coordinator of the Leadership Academy at Arizona State University.

JULIE Y. HUNGAR is vice chancellor of education and planning of Seattle Community Colleges.

WILLIAM H. WALLACE, JR., is director of human resources of the Center for Excellence in Teaching and Learning at Kennesaw State College.

RICHARD F. WELCH is interim director of the Center for Excellence in Teaching and Learning at Kennesaw State College.

Many faculty, administrators, and staff profit from leadership development opportunities afforded through institutional membership in multicampus programming that pools resources and opportunities for maximum individual and institutional benefit.

Programs Sponsored by Multicampus Systems, Consortia, Networks, and Associations

Sharon A. McDade, Kenneth E. Andersen, Frances L. White, Maria Santos

Interinstitutional cooperative efforts have created a number of interesting models of leadership development programming. These models take advantage of the synergy that bringing together similar institutions can provide to create leadership development opportunities of greater reach and depth than any individual member institution might be able to provide. Although the programming is similar to that found in individual institutions—internships, academies, and workshops—the models have greater complexity and breadth because of the interinstitutional relationships.

Several systems and consortia have established programs within this model. Three of these—the Committee for Institutional Cooperation, the Association of California Community College Administrators Mentor Program, and the California State University System Executive Leadership Development Program—are profiled here. In addition, the Colorado Exchange Program, which represents another model, is also described. A list of persons affiliated with the programs, with contact numbers, is provided in the Appendix.

CIC Academic Leadership Program

Kenneth E. Andersen

The Committee on Institutional Cooperation (CIC) is the academic consortium of the Big Ten Universities and the University of Chicago. The members

NEW DIRECTIONS FOR HIGHER EDUCATION, no. 87, Fall 1994 © Jossey-Bass Publishers

of the committee are the chief academic officers of their institutions. All members of the CIC (with the exception of the University of Chicago) have participated in the Academic Leadership Program. Participants have come from the Duluth Campus of the University of Minnesota and a full complement of fellows participates from the University of Illinois at Chicago.

The Academic Leadership Program (ALP), developed and sponsored by the Committee on Institutional Cooperation, completed its fifth year of operation in the academic year 1993–1994. The program has the capacity to serve forty-eight fellows annually, with four fellows named to the program by each of the respective campuses that hold membership in the CIC. The program has grown in numbers of fellows and member schools participating, with all CIC schools except the University of Chicago expected to participate in 1994–1995.

The program features a seminar series rotated among the participating campuses coupled with a variety of activities for the fellows on the individual campuses. The seminars provide a set of common experiences focused on current higher education issues while underlining both the similarities and differences in the cultures of the campuses, providing the opportunity for extensive interaction and networking among fellows and exposure to the key leaders of host institutions. However, there is great variety in the activities offered for fellows on the individual campuses, just as the emphases in and methods of selecting fellows vary widely.

The utility of this model for enhancing the development of academic leaders, both administrative and faculty, may be best understood through a description of the goals and conception of the program as envisioned during the planning stages; its evolution over the five years of its existence; and evaluative comments based on reactions of the fellows, campus liaisons, the coordinator, and CIC members. Though designed specifically to enhance the preparation of academic leaders for the Big Ten campuses, the model is applicable to institutions of varying types and aspirations.

The chief academic officers of the CIC meet periodically to discuss a range of issues of shared concern among their institutions. They have used a wide range of programs, such as those offered during the summers at Harvard, ACE fellowships, and programs targeting specific categories such as the Higher Education Resource Services (HERS)/Bryn Mawr program to enhance leadership by women. These programs have many advantages derived from an extended, intensive period of study and interaction with other participants. On the other hand, they are relatively expensive, limited in ability to serve more than one or two individuals from a campus, and often focus on a range of issues at highly differentiated institutions. A CIC-sponsored program that allowed greater numbers of participants, was limited in terms of time and money costs, and focused on leadership roles at CIC and similar institutions could be an worthwhile addition. Also, the program could identify participants from groups underrepresented in leadership roles, a major concern of the CIC.

Much of the initial impetus for developing the Academic Leadership Program came from Michigan State University with Robert Banks, currently assistant provost and assistant vice president for academic human resources, serving a major role in developing the idea, which he brought to the CIC through service on the planning committee and as ALP liaison for Michigan State. His record of participation is longer than that of any other individual associated with the program. Following preliminary discussion of the general idea, the CIC agreed that it had merit and called for a formal proposal to be developed by Indiana University, which was envisioned as the host campus for the first year of seminars. A planning committee drawn from five institutions of the CIC was responsible for detailed planning of the seminars, and conference staff at Indiana worked on issues of budget and facilities.

A variety of changes in the conception of the program occurred during the planning process. Originally, for example, involvement of a wide range of leaders in education was planned, with honoraria for the presenters and possible publication of a product. In time, this gave way to a more interactive focus with a wider variety of presentation styles and small-group sessions. Similarly, initial thought of four seminars gave way to plans for three; the year's seminars were to be rotated among the campuses. CIC personnel would receive only coverage of their expenses, and a two-day rather than three-day seminar format was established. The success of the lengthy planning process is suggested by the fact that the program is relatively unchanged in terms of the pattern ultimately designed.

Although it was originally intended to begin in the 1988–1989 academic year, the time needed for planning, the necessity of gaining final approval of the proposal, and the need for lead time to identify campus liaisons and fellows delayed the implementation of the program until the 1989–1990 academic year. Jean Girves, associate director of the CIC Office, served on the planning committee and coordinated the first year of the program, and Kenneth Andersen, then deputy vice-chancellor for academic affairs at the University of Illinois at Urbana–Champaign, assumed ALP coordination responsibilities starting in 1990–1991.

As described in the first promotional brochure, the primary object of the program was "to develop the leadership and managerial skills of faculty on CIC campuses who have demonstrated exceptional ability and administrative promise" (CIC, 1990). "Academic administrators at the CIC institutions have dual roles: They must be educational leaders and at the same time act as managers of large complex organizations. They are challenged by tightening budgets, changing student populations, and increasing pressures from external sources. To find creative, workable solutions to the problems that lie ahead, our universities must pay serious attention to leadership development. . . . The CIC Academic Leadership Program is specifically oriented to the challenges of academic administration at major research universities and is designed to help faculty members prepare to meet these challenges" (CIC, 1990).

The person designated as campus liaison is key to the success of the program at the individual campus level and a significant determinant of the number of fellows participating from the campus and their preparation for the seminars. The liaisons appointed by the chief academic officer of each campus are "responsible for all aspects of the Fellows' activities at their home institutions and for serving as campus contact with the CIC Office [the ALP Coordinator]. The liaisons are responsible for disseminating information about the program, establishing the selection procedures, identifying and assigning mentors, planning appropriate campus activities, and assisting in the planning and evaluation of the program" (CIC, 1990).

Liaisons typically have been associate provosts or others in academic affairs. Where liaisons are actively committed to the program, there is a diversity of campus activities and frequent participation by the liaison in the seminars as presenter, small group facilitator, and resource. Although the individual appointed may be an index of the commitment of the campus to the program, the liaison is clearly key to the success and, at times, to the continued participation of the campus in the program.

The selection process for fellows varies by campus. Typically, the selection is made in the late spring or summer. At some institutions, individuals apply for the program, are reviewed by a committee, and are interviewed. In other cases, individuals are nominated by deans or other administrators, with selection by the liaison or an administrative or faculty group. At one institution, recently appointed unit heads, typically department heads, are selected. Some limit selection to tenured faculty, others include administrators or professional staff. Most institutions give priority to people from groups underrepresented in administration. As the program has become more established, the number wanting to participate has grown.

The most typical campus activity is a series of meetings of fellows with various campus and (where appropriate) system administrators. Often, these sessions are tied to specific seminar topics. On some campuses, the fellows identify a project or are assigned a project to undertake for the year. Some integrate each year's fellows with prior fellows, with an emphasis on networking and sharing of experience and insights. Occasionally, fellows report back and share experiences with other groups. On some campuses, the liaison serves as or assists in identifying a mentor to meet with individual fellows, share experiences, assist in preparation for the seminars, and interact on a personal professional basis.

One focus of ALP activities for all fellows is the seminar series. Although there are changes in details and participants in every seminar, a basic pattern characterizes the year and the individual seminars. For the first four years of its existence, the seminar series featured three seminars on the topics of human resources, budgeting and long-range planning, and governance. Initially, the governance seminar was held first. However, the human resources seminar has been more successful as the initial seminar, and governance more effective as the culminating seminar. The budgeting and long-range planning seminar is the most successful in terms of participant response. Due to financial constraints, the number of seminars was reduced from three to two during the 1993–1994 academic year. The experiment of adding an extra half-day and of trying to integrate more material into the seminars resulted in some decline in what has been very high participant satisfaction and a loss in coverage of topics.

Fellows receive an announcement of the seminar with a general outline of the schedule approximately seven weeks in advance. Three weeks in advance, they receive a notebook containing background materials identified by the presenters, materials of particular value accumulated over the years, case studies, and items to be used during the seminar itself.

The seminars are focused on promoting interaction among the fellows. Following registration on a Thursday, the seminars begin with a buffet luncheon followed by a presentation by the host president or provost, who may address the seminar topic or provide an overview of issues and concerns of the campus or of higher education. The presentation is followed by a question-and-answer session of up to one hour. The remainder of Thursday, including an evening session, and the activities for Friday are given over to a variety of individual presentations, panels, and case studies. Emphasis is given to small-group sessions, often with reports shared and critiqued by the entire group. Saturday morning normally offers an open forum of provosts or other key administrative leaders from three different CIC institutions. To facilitate interaction, the membership of the small-group sessions is normally kept constant during a particular seminar but altered for each seminar. The entire group takes all meals together and the host institution sponsors a reception late Thursday evening. Friday evening features a dinner at a local restaurant or campus location with no scheduled evening program. An effort is made to provide time for individuals to become acquainted with the host campus (bus or walking tours) and some free time to meet colleagues on the campus.

A variety of methods are used to facilitate networking and interaction. Pictures and biographical sketches of the fellows are made available in a xeroxed version at the first seminar, and a more elaborate booklet is printed each spring that describes the program and the seminars and includes biographical sketches and photographs of the fellows. Addresses including fax and e-mail listings are distributed and updated at the time of each seminar.

Efforts to improve the seminar series involve evaluation forms mailed to all participants after each seminar and at the close of the year soliciting suggestions about future seminars and improvements in each seminar for the following year. At the time of the renewal of the program, after four years, all fellows were contacted and asked to assess the contribution of the program over time. Liaisons are also asked for their evaluation and suggestions after each seminar. Liaisons from the host institution are particularly helpful in identifying key individuals on their campuses to participate in panels and in arranging settings and presentations with key administrators.

To maintain a level of interaction, addresses of all previous fellows are updated annually and the revised list of fellows' titles, institutions, and addresses is mailed to every fellow. This mailing is accompanied by updates on the program and news likely to be of interest to the fellows. Some affinity groups that emerge over the course of the seminars remain in contact with each other in the years that follow.

From a variety of standpoints, the CIC Academic Leadership Program has been a success. The seminar series has been evaluated very favorably by the participants. Over time, their evaluations tend to become more positive. Several fellows held administrative appointments when they began the program. Others have moved into administrative positions, typically as a dean or into academic affairs or graduate school and research positions. Most have remained at the campus that identified them as a fellow, a few have moved within the CIC, and a few have taken positions at comparable institutions. Many individuals who have not moved into administrative roles have assumed major responsibilities in faculty governance. The knowledge of administrative roles and responsibilities has been identified as particularly helpful in making shared governance more functional.

One important contribution has been the growth of networking. Both during and after the fellowship years, individuals contact those they know to be working on particular problems or interested in particular areas and exchange information or obtain advice. The networks are used to identify potential hires and to identify possible new positions. Many participants have commented on the value of seeing how different institutions address the same issue and the value of learning how specific differences in campus cultures make for very different patterns of decision making and legitimation of the decisions. One key aspect for some institutions has been the growth of internal networking among the fellows on their own campus.

The program set as one goal increased participation in administration of underrepresented groups. An unexpected byproduct of having many such individuals as fellows has been a heightened awareness of the imperatives of a changed climate. With each seminar series, participants comment on the very different agenda and approach to issues that characterizes the seminars due to the diversity of participants. Several have commented on how different it feels to be a minority when one is used to being part of the unselfconscious majority. The combination of fellows is important: no one group is dominant. A group of all women, all minority faculty, or individuals selected solely on the basis of sexual preference would not provide the diversity and range of interaction that develops naturally during the seminars.

Another dimension of diversity arises out of the nature of the programming for the seminars. The forum periods provide the opportunity to see how the styles of administrators vary. At one seminar, for example, one provost spoke of the necessity of attending a vast number of social functions and ritual occasions, and another simply said that she limited her social schedule and did nothing in the evening. One president commented how much the family benefited from being involved in the presidential role; another said it was very hard on the family. The interaction afforded by the seminars adds markedly to an understanding of the differential weighting of factors as being costs or benefits of particular roles. Some report a change of career direction based on what they have learned about the limits of administrative roles whereas others view the possibilities more favorably than before.

Although renewed for another two-year period in 1993 after four years of operation, the number of seminars was cut from three to two to reduce costs. The seminar series has been quite successful in holding down costs. No speakers are compensated, although expenses are paid. Many members of the CIC have waived payment of expenses and express eagerness to be invited to future seminars. People drawn from the host campuses are not compensated.

The average cost per participant in the three-seminar series, excluding travel costs of the fellows to the seminars but including board and room and most costs associated with planning, execution, and support of the program, has averaged about $1,250. That cost is covered by the fellow's home institution. Some costs of mailings, xeroxing, and secretarial support have been absorbed by the University of Illinois.

An individual campus might attempt such a program on its own and succeeded to a modest degree. However, an individual campus cannot offer the benefit of the diversity of campus cultures or the range of presenters, including the key academic leaders. In a typical three-seminar series, a fellow hears and has the opportunity to question two or three presidents; eight or nine chief academic officers; several key administrators, ranging from university attorneys to affirmative action, sexual harassment, or student services personnel; several faculty governance leaders; and several experts in such areas as long-range planning and budgeting.

One criticism is that the program is seen as making a major contribution to the fellow, but it is unclear how the campus gains. Such questions typically arise on campuses that are not using on-campus activities for fellows as part of the program; the models used on other campuses could alter the perceptions that underlie this criticism. A further response is that developing leadership resources is a requirement for any viable entity.

The CIC Academic Leadership Program became possible because of the tradition of shared consultation and cooperative projects executed under the auspices of the CIC Office. Extensive planning resulted in significant changes in programming that yielded a program demanding relatively little change after the initial implementation. The program uses the expertise of the member institutions' faculty, staff, and key administrators at no cost to the program. The ultimate impact for the CIC institutions will not be known for several years, but the impact on the fellows and the movement into increased positions of responsibility both within the faculty role and in administrative roles suggest that the program is a cost-effective and promising tool for enhancing the quality of leadership available in coming years.

Association of California Community College Administrators (ACCCA)

Frances L. White

Over the past decade, mentoring has received increased recognition as a process that provides learning and skill development of a less experienced person through pairing with a more experienced person. Murray (1991) distinguishes what she calls a role model from a mentor. The role model may not know that she or he is being viewed as someone to emulate. In contrast, a mentor and protégé enter into an overt agreement to interact with the agreed-on goal of having the protégé learn and develop specific skills.

Organizations may choose a variety of approaches to stimulate organizational change, development, and growth, but structuring a mentor program that mandates participation will not result in any significant desired behavior change. In a voluntary program that emphasizes competence and commitment as characteristics to seek in recruiting qualified mentors, the credibility is high.

In keeping with the basic tenets of educating, nurturing, and "growing your own," the Association of California Community College Administrators, in recognition of the need to develop future leaders within the community college system, established a mentor program in 1988. The program was funded by a five-year grant from the Ford Foundation. Currently, the program is in its sixth year with more than one hundred individuals from ninety community colleges within California having participated. Their representation reflects a range of diversity in age, gender, and ethnicity. The program was designed to reflect the changing demographics of community college districts and to answer the call for new leadership (Valeau, Van Hook, and Spears, 1993).

The program's basic objectives are to enhance knowledge directly applicable to career success, identify the skills needed for upward mobility, develop a network of professionals in California, assist and offer training so that participants can become role models on campus, provide participants with an introduction to a visible network for career opportunities, develop strategies that contribute to a successful working relationship in a culturally diverse society, and encourage and provide support for working within the academic structure.

Furthermore, the ACCCA Mentor Program provides an invaluable year-long skills development program to its mentees. Each mentor–mentee pair works closely throughout the year, adhering to their mutually designed learning contract. The learning contracts developed between the mentor and mentee range in scope from completing research projects that design more efficient managerial systems in specific areas of college operations, to designing a career advancement program for the mentee to learn institutionwide planning and budget systems.

Each year, a letter is sent to community college chancellors, superintendents, presidents, and vice presidents inviting nominations for mentees and seeking volunteers to serve as mentors. An invitation is also sent to all community college administrators, who also apply for program participation as mentees. The selection process is based on formal applications, established criteria as determined by the Association of California Community College Administrators, and a review team made up of ACCCA commissioners and the program coordinator. Successful applicants are then paired with a mentor volunteer based on the mentee's stated goals and objectives, the mentor's stated interests and strengths, and geographical feasibility.

The mentors and mentees are invited to an orientation during the ACCCA Annual Conference, where specifics of the program are explained in detail. Program participants are also provided with the ACCCA Mentor Program Handbook, which serves as a guide to the mentoring relationship throughout the year.

During the year, the program coordinator works closely with each mentee and performs periodic checks on their progress. In addition, the program has special events. One event is the Annual Leadership Retreat, where the program participants spend two days in a relaxed environment learning about leadership and assessing their own leadership skills. Chief executive officers and other college administrators volunteer their time to discuss a variety of topics related to community college administration and leadership.

The second event occurs toward the end of the program year when the state chancellor's office hosts A Day with the Chancellor. This experience also gives the participants a better understanding of how community colleges function, as well as an overview of current issues and challenges facing the educational community today.

The program is evaluated annually by its participants via a formal evaluation instrument; each planned activity is also evaluated. The ACCCA Management Development Commission (MDC) reviews such evaluations and makes recommendations for improvement. The mentor program is under constant review that helps to sustain rigor and viability by incorporating evaluation feedback to make the program better. Moreover, most program participants find the annual events informative and meaningful. A number of graduates from the program have credited the program with their own professional success.

In a recent doctoral study endorsed by ACCCA (Majette-Daniels, 1993), prior mentors and mentees were surveyed on career and psychosocial functions of their mentoring experience. The findings support the benefits of such relationships, specifically on such dynamics as psychosocial mentoring benefits (such as role modeling, acceptance, counseling, and friendship), which were ranked as the highest achievements of the relationship. In terms of dynamics related to the career function (such as sponsorship, exposure, visibility, and coaching), achievement of these benefits revealed a lower degree of success. One explanation for the low ranking on the career function items was attributed to the geographical distance between mentee and mentor.

Another explanation appears to be related to the degree of satisfaction on certain psychosocial functions. In other words, individuals who really hit it off were more likely to receive certain career benefits. This may seem obvious because a certain amount of chemistry is essential to the success of any relationship.

As the ACCCA Mentor Program continues, a concentrated effort is being directed toward program improvement that will enhance training, pairing, institutional support, evaluation, and follow-up. Because the original grant has expired, ACCCA is now the primary source of financial support. This demonstration of support reflects ACCCA's commitment to improving educational leadership in California.

The current budget for the program is $5,000 per year, which is used to cover costs of mailings and various program activities. There is a program coordinator (nonsalaried) and a small group of volunteers who serve as program advisors.

Overall, the program has proven effective in promoting leadership skill development, professional growth opportunities, and administrative career options for individuals who choose to pursue a career in community college administration.

To highlight the program's success, here are a few comments from previous participants:

I strongly believe in the merits of this program and I would love to participate again.

The Mentor Program provided me with an excellent opportunity to candidly view the administrative and management styles, problems, and solutions of various personnel.

The rewards of mentoring are many. But nothing is more rewarding then watching and helping a younger colleague grow in self-confidence and understanding of community college administration.

My interaction with my mentor has been highly satisfying. I have had access to my mentor and I have been supported and encouraged.

One of the strengths of the program was the opportunity to have a sounding board to express some of my management concerns to someone who could be objective. The network with administrators outside of the campus has been very helpful to me.

The quality of the participants is very high. The mentees had a variety of experience and were very good candidates to progress up the career ladder. I am very pleased with my mentee.

My experience in the ACCCA Mentor Program has been most meaningful, educational, and interesting. My objectives were met and I had the chance to be exposed to more activities than I expected.

California State University System Executive Leadership Development Program

Maria Santos

The California State University Executive Leadership Development Program is a pilot program designed to provide selected individuals intensive executive learning experiences in a variety of settings throughout the California State University System, including the office of the chancellor, CSU Government Affairs in Sacramento, and CSU Federal Relations in Washington, D.C., as well as campus-based assignments. The executive fellows also attend the Harvard Institute for Educational Management or Management Development Program or other comparable development programs for executives in higher education and other conferences and workshops related to their professional objectives or scholarly interests. The assignments and development activities are regarded as training grounds for future CSU senior administrators.

The funding, the administrative support, and the publicity for the program are provided by the office of the chancellor. It is administered by the senior director for human resources and employee diversity, who reports directly to the vice chancellor for human resources. In addition to funds to support the professional development plan of each fellow, the chancellor's office reimburses the home campuses for the salary and benefits of each of the fellows while they are in the program.

The program was developed in response to the commitment by the Board of Trustees and the chancellor that The California State University assume a significant role in achieving diversity, and to the urgent need to develop a diversified pool of qualified candidates for executive positions in academic administration, campus presidencies, and senior positions at the system level. Because the number of potential positions at the executive level is limited and because of the expense involved in providing an individualized program of professional development for senior academic positions, the first two cycles of the program awarded four executive fellowships to the top candidates of a highly competitive process. Future cohorts may be further limited due both to the success in placing fellows in senior academic positions (lack of anticipated openings) and to budget constraints.

The highly competitive selection process begins with each campus president nominating two senior-level employees. Although preference is given to academic administrators, others exhibiting potential to succeed in senior management positions are accepted. Nominees are reviewed by a selection committee established by the chancellor, who makes final appointments.

The specific selection criteria for the executive fellows is based on the desired outcomes of the project. The pool of nominees therefore contains candidates with proven records of achievement in the CSU and strong potential for senior academic and executive positions. The ELDP is principally directed toward enriching the experiences of individuals whose interests and experience are in academic affairs; however, recognizing the large pool of talented persons in other areas, outstanding individuals from other appropriate divisions of the campuses are also identified. In addition to academic credentials and experience, it is also important that candidates have some administrative experience in higher education.

The program is evaluated annually to determine whether the desired outcomes were achieved. The first cycle was highly successful, resulting in the placement of a provost for academic affairs; a dean of arts, letters, and social sciences; and an associate provost for academic planning.

The strength of the program rests in its limited duration and objectives. It was consciously designed to immediately affect diversity at the highest policy levels of The California State University and worked backward from the selection criteria used to identify executives on the campus and system levels. Identifying candidates who possessed most of the desired qualifications and experiences, with specific areas that could reasonably be strengthened in a two-year fellowship, was the first step. The second step was to develop a personalized plan of professional development. The third step was, of course, introducing the executive fellows to potential employers on our various campuses and at the system level in situations that allow for evaluation and development of their administrative skills and their knowledge of the major issues facing higher education in this country and the CSU in particular. The final step is to provide assistance to each of the fellows in identifying potential positions and navigating the search process.

The major challenge has been funding. The fiscal crisis in the State of California has required several budget adjustments that have negatively affected the program.

Colorado Exchange

The Colorado Exchange provides yet another model of interinstitutional leadership development cooperation. Founded in 1990, the program is modeled after the National Faculty Exchange program. Its theme is "The exchange of knowledge is the genesis of opportunity." The exchange provides a unique avenue for "sharing knowledge and gaining new perspectives, and for enhancing skills and techniques" (Colorado Exchange, n.d.). Thirteen Colorado state colleges and universities participate. Exchanges exist for faculty, staff, and administrators, ranging from electricians, librarians, and accountants to English professors and associate academic deans.

Exchanges can be arranged "for a few hours, one day to one week, or longer depending on the goals and objectives of the exchange and the host campus" (Colorado Exchange, n.d.). Opportunities also exist to shadow (go to work with a counterpart) for a period of time at another institution. Faculty exchanges include providing a guest lecture to trading places for a semester or a year. Administrative exchanges can be direct or one-way, involve working on projects, sharing information and expertise, or gaining new experience at another institution. Annually, twenty to twenty-five people participated in the exchanges.

Campus liaisons disseminate applications. The application notes exchange site choices, placement parameters, and special considerations. Applicants selected for exchange receive an exchange planner that helps the candidate think through his or her participation in the program, the learning opportunities of the exchange, and any follow-up to the experience. Information on exchange sites and opportunities is regularly disseminated, as well as details on exchanges.

The exchange program is supported by an annual conference that focuses on issues of the workplace. The theme of the 1993 conference was "Empowerment: Winning in the Workplace." The two-day conference provided additional opportunities for exchange participants to interact, share ideas, and develop new management and leadership skills.

Currently, the exchange is going through a transition. Karen Earley, the director of faculty and staff development, reported to the vice president for academic affairs at the University of Colorado when she started the program. In recent institutional cutbacks, she was reassigned to the dean of the school of education. She took administration of the program with her, but must find new funding to pay for it (Earley, personal communication, December 1993).

Conclusion

The models described in this chapter demonstrate the wide variety of programming available to institutions that choose to cooperate in leadership development. Despite the variety, all share the common belief that institution-specific leadership development can be enhanced through the shared resources and pooled opportunities of many institutions of similar types, missions, and interests. Costs can be kept down while interaction opportunities can be enhanced through a synergy of cooperation.

References

Colorado Exchange. "Program Brochure." Boulder: University of Colorado, n.d.
Committee on Institutional Cooperation. *Academic Leadership Program 1989–1990*. Urbana: University of Illinois Press, 1990.

Majette-Daniels, B. "Mentoring Effectiveness in the Association of Community College Administrators (ACCCA) Mentoring Program." Ed.D. dissertation, University of San Francisco, 1993.
Murray, M. *Beyond the Myths and Magic of Mentoring: How to Facilitate an Effective Mentoring Program.* San Francisco: Jossey-Bass, 1991.
Valeau, E. J., Van Hook, D., and Spears, S. "Mentoring Model for Use on Local Campuses." *ACCCA Mentor Program Handbook.* Long Beach, Calif.: Association of California Community College Administrators, 1993.

SHARON A. MCDADE is assistant professor of higher education administration and principal adviser of the Higher Education Administration Graduate Programs at Teachers College, Columbia University.

KENNETH E. ANDERSEN is professor of speech communication at the University of Illinois at Urbana–Champaign. He is also campus liaison and coordinator of the Academic Leadership Program for the Committee on Institutional Cooperation.

FRANCES L. WHITE is assistant dean of instruction for communications, art, and physical education at Laney College of the Peralta Community College District and coordinator of the Association of California Community College Administrators Mentor Program.

MARIA SANTOS is senior director of human resources and employee diversity and director of the Executive Leadership Development Program of the California State University.

Training and development programs directed to staff represent an institutional investment in the skills and careers of nonacademic personnel.

Staff Training and Development Programs

Phyllis H. Lewis, Jamie C. Cavalier, Rosalyn Hantman, William F. Waechter, Allan H. Yamakawa

During the last decade, many colleges and universities have more actively acknowledged the role of staff employees in accomplishing institutional goals. Sometimes, this recognition has focused on the significant costs of staff salaries and benefits. In many cases, campus leaders have begun to see staff persons as both actors and receivers in the educational enterprise, not merely as fringe players. For example, student retention activities frequently focus on the role of staff in interacting with students. Staff development, then, makes good sense from a management perspective because it can have a positive effect on outcomes.

Something else is at work, however. Nonacademic personnel are typically attracted to educational institutions because of the expectation that the institution will care about them more than would an employer in the private sector. When they feel disappointed in that expectation, low morale results. Raising their voices, sometimes alongside faculty and students, staff persons are demanding more attentiveness to issues such as career development. In some cases, the response has been formal ongoing programming that, in effect, identifies the educational and even career development needs of staff as the legitimate interest of the institution. These programs can serve as catalysts for global strategies to enhance leadership capabilities for personnel at all levels.

Although many institutions have such programs, four have been selected here for the purposes of illustration. The Employee Development Program of The University of North Carolina at Greensboro, begun in 1990, has moved through several phases; it began with training only, and now has become somewhat active in organizational development activities. In its latter role, it has great potential for exercising long-term influence on the overall administration of the institution. A much older program at the University of Illinois at Chicago has significant staffing and funding. Its roots were in the organization development context, with management and supervisory training added to enhance its primary work. Columbia University's program is also a mature one with a broad mission, but it does not operate with nearly the full-time staff and budget as some other similar programs; instead it has relied on Columbia faculty, administrators, and even graduate students, as well as outside consultants, to offer a wide range of training and development programs. Employee development programming at Maricopa County Community College District in Arizona is an example of how an existing development function has been improved through initiatives in total quality management.

University of North Carolina at Greensboro's Employee Development Program

Phyllis H. Lewis

The initiation of an employee training program in 1990 was the last step in the overall plan, which began implementation three years earlier, to transform the human resource function at the University of North Carolina at Greensboro (UNCG) into a more influential player in senior administration. Until the late 1980s, the human resources (HR) unit was a minor processing and record-keeping center with little opportunity to change the institutional culture.

The vice chancellor for business affairs, to whom the office of human resources reported, had a vision for the development of better managers for the university, who he believed were ill-prepared for their supervisory assignments. The problem had become painfully clear in the acceleration of employee–management conflicts and the increase in complaints that resulted in internal grievances and Equal Employment Opportunity Commission filings. Shortly after a senior human resources officer was brought on board to head the expanded human resources unit, a position was set aside for a training director. The principal mission during the training program's inception was to teach the necessary skills, including effective communication, for improving relationships among employees and between employees and their supervisors. The measure of success would be in whether there was a real decrease in the number and intensity of workplace conflicts.

With this as her essential charge, the new director of training began to develop a programmatic approach to the training function. It was essential that the program be tied closely into the fabric of other human resources functions. One of three people who reported to the associate vice chancellor for human resources, the director of training became a full member of the HR management team. This reporting arrangement allowed her to integrate her own ideas about training and presentation approaches with the actual needs of the client base.

Gathering information was the first step in setting up the program. The first stop was among HR staff, who had experience with typical issues that would be responsive to training. Staff members in employee relations and position management provided data about the areas of greatest concern among employees and supervisors. For example, a number of recent grievances had related to disputes about the use of overtime. Others involved interpretations of the disciplinary procedures. Permeating the many complaint situations was the general lack of skill in handling conflict situations. In cooperation with other HR staff, the director of training compiled a list of policies and state regulatory documents that should be required reading for supervisors.

Key people from on campus were also interviewed for their views on how the training program should be structured and what issues it should address. A number of staff, faculty, and administrators participated in focus groups. This first step in the startup process, the needs analysis, served several purposes. It helped to market the program by making people aware of what was to occur, and it helped to secure buy-in. In fact, word-of-mouth, grass-roots promotion of the program occurred before the first workshop was designed. Other kinds of support were being secured among top administrators. The associate vice chancellor for human resources sought the opinion and investment of her colleagues. A structure for maintaining such feedback and support was eventually formalized as a training advisory committee that represented all constituents of the program.

Although the information gathered to this point prepared the way for actual course content, certain other pieces were necessary for the training function to have a programmatic structure. The courses could not be merely a shotgun approach. Thus, the training director attempted to learn as much as possible about similar programs in other universities. Using the membership listings of the American Society for Training and Development and the College and University Personnel Association, she identified institutions that were likely to have significant training functions and sent each institution a survey instrument. The questionnaire requested information about course content, use of off-the-shelf versus internally developed materials, course attendance requirements, methods of publicity and evaluation, annual budget and staff, and support materials such as publications and conferences for the training function. The survey stage, which produced excellent results, also created a basis for a network of people who have become important to the UNCG training function over the years.

The next step in setting up the employee training program was to make explicit the university's commitment to the activity. This step involved frequent discussions between the chancellor and his direct associates. One topic that was considered was whether participation in a training program should be formally recognized in considering internal applicants for promotions. Other points requiring discussion at this level were whether there should be a direct charge to individuals or departments and what the university's position should be regarding time away from work for staff employees.

During the early stages of the program, there was no mention of requiring attendance for individuals or a class of employees; in fact, those who were closely involved believed that to do so would be a real detriment in the academic environment. Instead, the program was set up as completely voluntary; however, there were considerable efforts by the director of training, the associate vice chancellor for human resources, and the vice chancellor for business affairs to sway managers of large units toward mandatory participation, especially for topic areas where grievances and complaints were common.

A more direct approach to securing management support for a training activity was used when the unit head initiated or agreed in principle to some specifically targeted training. The assumption, which was borne out during the last four years, was that the effectiveness of the training experience would be directly linked to the degree of management support. Thus, the director of training developed an explicit agreement, to be signed both by her and by the head of the requesting unit, that specifies the objective to be accomplished and the kinds of support to be provided by the unit during and after the training, and allows the requesting unit to recommend format, place, time, and scope of the training.

The information on campus concerns indicated a clear need for the training program to address communication skills, supervisory skills, and diversity concepts. The issue of sexual harassment and other aspects of affirmative action were at the top of the list. Other identified needs included training on interviewing and other aspects of the hiring process, implementation of the university's performance management program, problem solving and dispute resolution, the disciplinary process for classified staff employees, position classification, the workers' compensation program, and compensation issues, especially application of the Fair Labor Standards Act. In addition, customer service, team building, personal financial planning, time management, CPR, and first aid were identified as preferred components of the total employee development program.

After determining which course offerings should occur first, the training staff reviewed approaches for individual courses. For some topics, such as sexual harassment, vendor-offered programs were purchased. However, there was a general assumption that programs not specifically produced for a university environment would need to be carefully tailored and used in combination with materials developed in-house. The theory that programs are not particularly effective if they do not relate well to real-life situations applies emphatically in the university setting. People tend to be insulted, for example, with scenarios that take place in a corporate setting. In preparing some courses, the training staff engaged communication specialists and scriptwriters to produce videos based on actual situations for UNCG. For example, video for a program on dispute resolution depicted a supervisor and an employee discussing a situation that had actually taken place; also, the program on sexual harassment, prepared for faculty audiences, included a brief video of a respected faculty member addressing her colleagues about the role of good communication in preventing sexual harassment concerns among students.

During the first two years of the program, a number of courses were offered to address the particular needs of the campus. A brochure was developed along the lines of a college catalogue, which was distributed twice a year to all faculty and staff. Particular programs were marketed through the human resources newsletter. Other forms of marketing included the posting of banners and posters for special events and special invitations to targeted audiences. As the program gained acceptance, a number of unit heads requested specialized training sessions for their employees. For example, the director of the office of financial aid requested that the six-module course on leadership be delivered to that unit's supervisory personnel. Some of the programs were delivered specifically for staff in the physical plant department, which had been the locus of an excessive number of employee–supervisor conflicts.

In designing particular training courses and workshops, the training staff relied on principles of adult education. Programs must be interesting, with a minimum amount of lecture, and must be nonthreatening. The main theme is variety—videotapes, case studies, modeling, role plays, group processing, and experiential exercises have all been used. Abundant handout materials are usually associated with each workshop. One method that has become especially important in later offerings focusing on team building is the use of self-discovery instruments. These include the Myers–Briggs Type Indicator (MBTI), the Fundamental Interpersonal Relations Orientation-Behavior (FIRO-B), and the Kirton Adaption–Innovation Inventory.

The above comments have summarized the early years of the training program at UNCG. During late 1992, the program began to be less reactive to problems; to some extent, this change may have been evidence of its own success. The decrease in employee–supervisory conflicts had been noticed by unit heads, who, in turn, were eager to have the training staff lead conflict-preventive activities. The shift was toward a more organizational development approach. The influence of the training program has been widely felt in areas of the campus that are not generally receptive to human resource theory. Several faculty departments invited the director of training to conduct team-building sessions for academic personnel. That process had been at work previously with regard to staff reorganizations.

Another development involving faculty was a vote by the faculty government body recommending that a health promotion program be established for the campus and that it be set up within the office of human resources. That program was eventually assigned to the training function and corresponded well with the emphasis by the program on the total well-being of the individual employee.

A decision was made in late 1992 to change the name of the program to Employee Development in order to reflect the developmental approach. Rather than being merely a vehicle for fixing specific problems on campus, which had been the rationale for its inception, the revised program had earned its way into an identification with the central educational mission of the university. The 1993–1994 period has seen the program self-consciously emphasize that new mission. Its message is a positive one, deliberately transmitted to help build self-esteem among faculty and staff and to enhance the overall work of the university. For example, in speaking at an award ceremony for housekeepers, the director of training, as guest speaker, led an exercise that teaches the relationship of housekeeping with the reason everyone is at the university—its students. The task of breaking down barriers between groups on campus—demonstrated first in its delivery of isolated programs about better communication, the need to recognize and value personal differences, and responsiveness to customer needs—has become an important and pervasive enhancement for the university's obligations to both its employees and its students.

University of Illinois at Chicago's Training and Organization Development Program

Allan H. Yamakawa

In 1973, the training function at the University of Illinois at Chicago Circle was eliminated because of budget reallocations. It remained shut down until 1979, when a new vice chancellor for administration, in response to requests from the classified staff, reopened the position of director of training and staff development. The person selected to head this function had been director of training services for an international training and management consulting group.

The first effort was an institutionwide needs assessment, which revealed a distressingly high level of insularity, interunit competition, and intraunit conflict, as well as a clear need for supervisory and management staff training and team building. However, some units resisted having these organizational issues addressed, particularly by a staff development department whose mission they perceived as being solely that of improving staff proficiency.

With these challenges, the new director went to his boss and told him that he needed a "bigger gun"—a title and mission that would enable him to go into units and offer organizational intervention, management consultation, and long-range services. The result was a new name for the unit: Organizational Development.

Over the next several years, the office of organizational development provided services to the University at Chicago Circle as well as the University of Illinois at the Medical Center, also located in Chicago, and the University of Illinois at Urbana–Champaign. During the reorganization of the university in 1982, which merged the Chicago Circle and Medical Center campuses, the office of organization development played a supporting role; for example, it facilitated mergers of counterpart units from the two campuses.

The office itself was combined with the training and development section of the personnel services office on the Medical Center campus to form the unit that remains in place today as the office of training and organization development. Over the years, this unit has absorbed other training and organization development (T&OD) functions that had previously been fragmented in various other units. For example, campus auxiliary services and physical plant transferred responsibilities and salary lines to the centralized function.

With an annual budget from the state and indirect cost-recovery funds of approximately $200,000, the T&OD unit is able to provide its programs free to its users. Exceptions include highly specialized programs, for which development time is charged, and programs in which external instructors are used, such as computer productivity training. Services requested by units from other University of Illinois campuses, where there is no comparable function available, are provided on a fee-for-services basis.

The unit consists of a director, associate director (who is responsible for staff development and general training programs), an administrator, a registrar and training support specialist, three internal consultants, one training officer, and student assistants. Its physical facilities include a large, modern training room equipped with video projection and electronic chalkboard, a smaller conference room, a food-service area, an audio–visual engineering studio, storage facilities, private offices, and shared spaces.

Currently, the office of training and organization development divides its resources about equally among four functions: management and supervisory training, staff development, management consulting, and organization development services. Except for the staff development programs, which are driven by campus needs and learner interests, these functions are aimed chiefly toward changing the campus organizational culture from one of intergroup competition to one of collaboration and empowerment.

The Management and Supervisory Development Series includes courses on the academic as boss, a senior management seminar, a program on strategic and tactical planning, and a seven-day program on the supervision fundamentals, which is required for all newly hired or promoted supervisors. Topics covered in these programs include communication, conflict resolution, planning, resource management, time management, selection interviewing, performance management, and employee evaluation. In some cases, participants receive orientation to the civil service system, collective bargaining, and state and federal legislation affecting human resource management. In addition, these programs contain elements that support the campus's commitment to total quality management. There is a special focus on building trust, teamwork, leadership, change management, collaborative management, and subordinate empowerment. Particular emphasis is placed on the nature and sources of power, the role of trustworthiness in achieving and maintaining influence and authority, communication skills, and leadership behaviors.

Where these development programs end, management consulting and organization development services begin. Site-specific implementation considerations, strategic planning, contingency planning, problem prevention planning, systems design, conflict management, and similar services are available to supervisors and managers. Although consulting services are available to any supervisor, manager, or administrator, most clients tend to have been initiated to concepts of organization development during participation in a training program. Consulting relationships may include self-study approaches, action-planning consultation, and coaching.

The office of training and organization development also provides unit-based services that may include targeted training, team building, role negotiation, strategic planning, conflict resolution, and organizational renewal. Group size for unit-based services has been as small as two and as large as eighty in one setting. One unit, comprising 2,000 employees, participated in a series of connected seminars.

The typical two- or three-day team-building intervention begins with an exercise that seeks to align the unit mission with the campus mission and goals and to relate the unit mission to individual goals and objectives. After obstacles and improvement targets are identified, action planning begins with checkpoint dates and the assignment of accountability.

During the team-building intervention, discussions attempt to identify conflicts and overlap and to develop the notion of individual value added for consumers of the unit's services. To give insights into the role of personal style in creating interpersonal stress, instruments such as the Personal Profile and the Thomas–Kilmann Conflict Style Inventory are used. These help develop understanding and clarify nomenclature for discussions of the role of individual style in defining, communicating, and maintaining one's positions. Sometimes participants see how their own styles cause them to act uncooperatively when opposed and to resist reasonable alternatives.

An example of a team-building exercise used during the intervention is as follows: each person is asked to communicate a request, a complaint, and an affirmation to each other person in the group by completing these statements: "I would like you to do the following more or better, because . . ."; "I would like you to do the following less or not at all, because . . ."; and "I appreciate it when you do the following because. . . ." These statements are handed to the other participants. The recipients, one by one, read the statements received from the others, acknowledge the statements, and then make, or decline to make, commitments to comply with the requests. Discussion, questions, clarification, and other communication are permitted and even encouraged.

The team-building intervention ends with setting follow-up dates for a review of progress on action plans and on interpersonal issues. Individual consultation is offered as members of the team work through their portions of the action plans.

All management and supervisory training, consulting services, and unit interventions are assessed in multiple ways. The two most important are the degree to which the training, service, or intervention contributes to the improvement the unit sought and the dollar value of the improvement. The office of training and organization development attempts to focus the attention of clients and the campus on both the cost and the value of training and organization development services. Although services of the unit are generally provided at no cost to the receiving participant or unit, the T&OD unit does require, as a form of consideration, agreement that participants will develop improvement projects as the result of their experience. Generally there is a follow-up report back to T&OD about the outcome of that project. T&OD, in turn, is able to compute a value-added figure for assessing its own worth to the institution. For example, for a problem that results in remediation, as opposed to terminating a troublesome employee, legal counsel will provide a dollar cost for the termination that does not occur. This amount represents dollars saved because of T&OD's intervention. By computing added value to the university, T&OD measured its worth as more than twenty times the cost of maintaining the department.

The office of training and organizational development reports to the associate vice chancellor for human resources, who reports to the vice chancellor for administration and human resources. There is a less direct relationship to the university director of human resources, the corporate officer responsible for human resources at the central administration level in Urbana–Champaign.

Columbia University's Department of Training and Development Programs

Rosalyn Hantman

Columbia University (CU) is a major urban research and teaching institution consisting of fifteen schools and numerous administrative departments, institutes, and research centers based at several campus locations. The office of training and development is the only centrally based unit within the university that supports the training needs of a noninstructional employee population of approximately 7,500 individuals. This is a considerable challenge because only one professional staff member, the director, and one support individual, the training coordinator, have been budgeted to support the full range of services provided to the university community.

Because of its minimal staffing and budget allocations, creating a meaningful employee training and development program at Columbia University has required creativity and resourcefulness. The key to its successes has been the building of bridges to tap the wealth of resources within the university community. Relationships with faculty and administrators have been cultivated to provide numerous leadership and employee development experiences at either minimal or no cost to participants or their sponsoring schools and departments. In addition, the program relies on graduate students and consultants from outside the university and employs train-the-trainer methods to broaden program delivery.

The office of training and development coordinates the efforts of all those recruited as presenters and facilitators and promotes these programs to university administrators. In addition, the training director has recently developed partnerships with a number of CU continuing education departments to offer employees access to continuing education programs at a fraction of the publicly advertised program costs. This includes computer training as well as a variety of executive development residential seminars and short courses.

The director of training and development has had a relatively free hand in determining what programs to offer and how to structure and deliver them. The program has benefited from information received through informal benchmarking efforts with peer institutions that are more fully staffed and funded. A series of training programs was developed that, with internal training resources, could be presented quickly and effectively. In addition, many programs and services were developed in response to direct requests from senior management for training on specific topics. Currently, a training needs assessment has been initiated to more clearly evaluate the full range of training and professional development priorities across schools and administrative departments at all campus locations. Future programs will more closely target critical priorities based on the assessment results.

The office of training and development's public seminars, workshops, and forums for university personnel fall generally into the following subject areas: leadership development, supervisory training, computer training, quality service, diversity-related programs, administrative training, and health and safety promotion. These areas are described in subsequent paragraphs.

• Management and leadership development programs have included the Middle Management Development Program, which has now been offered for seven consecutive years with some variation occurring each year, and the new CU Leadership Series: Leadership and Change. Typically these are instructor-led, meeting for half-day sessions for eight to ten weeks. All faculty are from the Graduate School of Business. The thirty participants per series are middle- to senior-level administrators from a variety of campus locations. Extensive handouts include articles and case studies, presession reading assignments, and other materials as assigned. The office of training and development initiates, develops, and markets the program. T&D staff recruit faculty and coordinate the curriculum to create organized syllabi, prepare faculty handouts, and coordinate extensive administrative details.

Other programs on the theme of management and leadership development have included Conflict Resolution, Developing Team Performance, and Managing and Leading in Leaner Organizations. These courses have been taught by faculty from Teachers College, the School of Social Work, and the School of Business.

• Each semester, T&D offers university supervisors opportunities to participate in a supervisory training program, developed to enhance a supervisor's core interpersonal skills and to support his or her ability to manage individual performance. These are led by a certified trainer. The program series meets for half-day sessions, once each week for up to eight weeks. A maximum of eighteen people participate in each series. The program can be implemented as a "public" program, with enrollment from a large variety of departments and schools, or as a custom program at the request of individual deans and vice presidents. All sessions are highly interactive and emphasize discussion and group and individual practice for new skills. Media include handouts on skill topics and a video showing examples of supervisor–subordinate interactions. T&D determines specific program segments, provides overviews of program to participants' managers to generate support, and handles correspondence, registration, and other administrative details.

Other programs under the theme of management and supervision include Addressing Discrimination in the Workplace, Sexual Harassment, Working with Persons with Disabilities, Managing Performance and Other Problems in the Workplace, Employee Absenteeism, and Performance Communication and Appraisal. These programs typically consist of a single two- or three-hour session. Instructors are usually drawn from the administrative office with responsibility for the function or program topic.

• Computer training opportunities for university employees have expanded significantly during the current fiscal year. T&D has partnered with the Division of Continuing Education to create the Computer Training Initiative for the Columbia Community (CTICC), a program that provides computer applications training to university faculty and staff for a fraction of the original public program cost. Employees may now participate in instructor-led courses that meet their computing needs in locations convenient to their worksites. This program made computer training more accessible to CU employees. In addition, T&D has recently introduced self-paced multimedia computer training technology to the Columbia community. A wide range of computer training applications are now offered, providing a somewhat more cost-effective alternative to instructor-led courses. The T&D office is equipped with two CD-ROM computer stations, and in one month has trained sixty employees in one administrative department. T&D is currently promoting this technology in other campus locations.

• T&D has participated in a consortium of college and university personnel officers in the New York metropolitan area in order to negotiate a volume discount for the purchase of training materials for in-service customer service training. T&D provides train-the-trainer services to help schools and departments develop their own in-house implementation of this type of program. Sessions are designed to run for a half day, once each week for three consecutive weeks. These programs were originally produced for support personnel, but experience has found them to be more successful in groups consisting of officers and staff of a work unit. Because group interaction is key, it is generally more productive to limit participation to fifteen participants per group. Each participant receives a participant manual; the complete program uses a set of three video cassettes, providing participants with examples of customer-service interactions. An enhancement of this program delivered to one department featured a custom video, reinforcing its relevance to this organization.

• A number of programs designed to promote sensitivity around the issues of multiculturalism at Columbia have been offered. These programs have generally been instructor-led; they include East and West at Columbia and Hispanic Cultural Values in the Workplace. Typically, seminars are conducted as a half-day or all-day session. As with most programs sponsored by T&D, participation has been voluntary for these seminars, and often reaches those already sensitized to concerns relating to diversity. An alternative approach would be to have the senior manager in an organization strongly encourage participation of all employees in his or her area. T&D has also purchased a number of instructional videos in support of diversity, especially workplace diversity. These videos can be viewed by individuals, but training goals are best served when there is a facilitator-led discussion. The training office initiates programs, recruits speakers, sets up participant groups, handles administrative details, and evaluates materials, videos, and consultants.

• A number of administrative programs are conducted each semester to communicate CU policies, systems, processes, and procedures to employees. New programs are frequently introduced; others are often reworked. Programs have been designed for the controller and treasury applications, human resource processing, gifts, internal audit, purchasing, and printing. These sessions are led by subject experts or administrators who have responsibility for each of these functions. Single sessions are offered with parallel schedules at a number of campus locations. Both administrators and support personnel attend. Some basic programs are geared specifically to new users; others target more experienced users. Sessions vary in enrollment between fifteen and seventy people, depending on the topic. These sessions provide extensive handouts (charts, forms, contact lists, and manuals). Overhead transparencies and slides are often used. An interactive session on internal controls, presented by representatives of the CU internal audit department, has recently been videotaped. Plans to deliver other videotaped CU administrative training programs are underway. T&D organizes and develops programs, assists administrators with structure for sessions and with preparation of handouts and transparencies, and coordinates correspondence, registration, confirmation notes, room assignments, and scheduling.

• A wide variety of health promotion and university safety instructional programs have been offered, using the services of CU administrators and faculty and speakers from not-for-profit organizations such as the American Cancer Society and the New York Lung Association. Typically, such programs are offered at the noon hour, providing easy access to all interested personnel. Large numbers of support personnel and officers have enrolled in these programs.

They are offered at no cost to the participants or the university. T&D initiates, organizes, and promotes the program series, recruits and coordinates speakers and programs; and handles correspondence and administrative details.

In addition to courses and workshops in these seven areas, T&D also compiles and distributes listings of training resources that are provided by other CU organizations. Such listings have included training offered by academic information systems for computing classes, student financial information services for financial aid seminars, physical education for gym classes, and the employee benefits office for benefits orientation programs.

T&D has begun to offer alternative instructional media though videotaped administrative training and through CD-ROM interactive programs for computer applications. An expansion of this self-paced training technology will provide a cost-effective alternative to more traditional forms of instruction. The CU training function is currently in transition; a number of internal and external forces will affect its new direction and focus. The university president has convened a task force to evaluate the current structure and delivery of student services. Its recommendations and outcomes may well call for renewed emphasis on customer service training programs for all employees in student contact offices. Should resources be provided to support a consistent and integrated service program, customized service provider training will be developed and delivered specifically for select employee groups.

Results of the universitywide training needs assessment administered earlier in the year are expected to influence future directions. Those needs, prioritized and articulated by senior and mid-level administrators, will drive decisions regarding program development.

Maricopa County Community College District's Employee Development Program

Jamie C. Cavalier, William F. Waechter

In November 1991, Paul A. Eisner, chancellor of the Maricopa County Community College District (MCCCD), presented his vision of the future to a large number of Maricopa colleagues. Three months later, a group representing faculty, managers, and support staff became the Commission on Quantum Quality. The commission received a mandate from the chancellor to investigate total quality management (TQM) programs in community colleges, universities, the government, and industry. The chancellor believed that although Maricopa has already attained national recognition for its innovative programs, adopting the tenets of TQM might produce "quantum" advancements for the district. The commission presented its recommendations to the chancellor in August 1992. The governing board accepted the report in September. Thus, a quality-improvement philosophy was adopted by the district.

Some significant changes took place immediately: the title of the vice chancellor of human resources was changed to vice chancellor, quality and employee development to reflect the shift in emphasis; the Quantum Quality Executive Council (Districtwide Steering Team) was appointed. This decision-making body is responsible for implementing the quality improvement effort across the ten colleges, the Maricopa Skill Center, and District Support Services Center.

As the quality initiative was beginning to take hold, the district experienced a funding shortfall. All departments in the colleges and central office cut budgets to meet new spending limits. Although this situation caused much consternation, it also provided MCCCD with the challenge to meet lowered budgets without having impact on programs or services to students and the community. Thus, it became imperative that quality-based planning provide long-term solutions and not dwell on quick fixes. As part of this new introspection, current professional development programs for employees began to be reviewed. The district had consistently appropriated considerable financial and human resources to professional development activities and programs for all employees, but the efforts were not necessarily consistent, integrated, or coordinated.

Employee interviews were conducted throughout the organization to assess the current and future needs of employees. Although time-consuming, this method of obtaining information proved to be the most appropriate and effective in obtaining direct employee feedback. Sixteen common development areas emerged as being central and critical to an effective employee development program. It also became evident that employee development should be broadened. Programs were needed that would provide flexible, career-long opportunities that could ensure job skill enhancement, increased knowledge, depth in expertise, worthwhile experience, and improvement of well-being and health; these needs would challenge MCCCD's human potential. It was also evident that it was necessary to tap into internal expertise to accomplish these goals, given the imposing budget restrictions.

During the employee interviews, the areas most often mentioned as desirable by employees were a comprehensive new employee orientation program that would acculturate new employees to MCCCD's operational environment and procedures; a comprehensive approach to employee well-being and health; and coordinated job-enhancement opportunities that created a progressive framework for advancement. Examples given were internships, advanced job skills training, apprenticeship programs, job exchanges, and mentoring. Hence, based on employee input, these areas became the beginning priorities.

Beginning in January 1994, new employee orientation was expanded from a three-and-a-half-hour program to one-and-a-half days. Sessions now include the usual welcome, overview of the history and organization of MCCCD, and flexible benefits sign-up, as well as sessions on quantum quality awareness, equal employment opportunity, affirmative action, sexual harassment, and budgeting. A half-day sign-up for MCCCD's flexible benefits finishes out the initial orientation.

During the first eighteen months of employment, new employees are required to attend two additional orientation sessions. The first, an electronic communication workshop that focuses on electronic mail and MCCCD's telephone system, is held regularly on-site at the colleges; the second is an informational session focusing on nonhealth-related employee benefits. The informational session is broadcast over MCCCD's video-conferencing network to eliminate travel time and offer convenience and availability. The topics presented are tuition waivers, reimbursement accounts, transportation programs, wellness, and an overview of the employee policy group structure and manuals. Employee interaction is encouraged. Thus, this more comprehensive orientation program helps new employees to adapt more quickly and easily to MCCCD's culture and environment.

As the process of program evaluation for cost reduction and containment continued, the office of organizational wellness was identified as one where the impact of the program could be maintained and continued with reorganization and realignment, thus eliminating the need for a separate department. In July 1993, Maricopa's wellness initiative was reestablished. Using high-quality processes and tools, the districtwide health-risk assessment, incorporating health counseling into the evaluation, is being implemented as the result of a partnership arrangement with CIGNA, MCCCD's health insurance carrier. Second, a wellness lending library has been organized and is available to all students and the community through the Phoenix metropolitan area network of on-line catalogs, including the MCCCD college libraries, local university libraries, and city libraries. Third, a model MCCCD–health carrier partnership has been established to meet customer needs and expectations of both organizations by offering on-site health services and education.

Another important result of the quality improvement approach was the improvement to VISIONS, a long-standing program of staff internships. In response to a 1984 employee development survey, the VISIONS internship program was created to identify career opportunities within the district. Over the years, it has evolved to provide opportunities for retraining and job enhancement. In fiscal year 1993, VISIONS became a regular budget item, allowing for long-term planning. VISIONS funding is used for personnel replacement costs only. To stretch VISIONS dollars, employees are encouraged to be as creative as possible in their funding solutions. It is typical for the department or college of the intern to contribute funding as well as the receiving department or college. This arrangement establishes a three-way commitment to the professional development of the individual.

The consistent weakness of the VISIONS program for most employees was the identification of a potential mentor. Now, rather than employees acting in isolation, the VISIONS internship program has evolved to where it matches and connects potential employee interns with potential mentors. A process was established in 1992–1993 that asks an employee to develop a list of current skills, the desired internship content area, and preferred internship location.

Any faculty member or supervisor who is interested in being a mentor is asked to submit similar information concerning a potential intern. Potential interns are then connected with potential mentors in areas meeting those criteria. It is the responsibility of a potential mentor and intern to determine whether an actual internship is possible. The maximum time length of an internship is one fiscal year. There is no minimum time. This matching program was an immediate success and has doubled in participation.

Employees are encouraged to explore two other design options. The traditional internship involves an employee seeking out a mentor in a desired area relying on the employee's own work contacts and professional network. Another design option is the domino. Here, an employee applies for an internship. The replacement for the employee is another employee at a lower salary grade who would also be a VISIONS intern. If possible, a third employee replaces the second employee, and so on. Thus, costs for all internships are reduced to one replacement cost at the lowest salary level.

Future expansion of the VISIONS internship program is being planned to allow employees to pursue opportunities in other ways, both internal and external to Maricopa. Much interest has been expressed in establishing a pool of interns that would be available for project internships. These would be variable in length and occur throughout the year. Also, there are discussions exploring the possibilities of local university–community college internship exchanges. Such internships would allow employees of both organizations to interact as mutual customers, learning about processes and how to improve them for the betterment of MCCCD mutual customers, the student, and the community.

The use of quality improvement processes and techniques for employee development activities has largely shifted the recognition of expertise from external consultants to internal employees. Tapping into Maricopa's diverse workforce has encouraged a broader recognition and appreciation for internal expertise and a greater resolve and confidence in solving internal employee development dilemmas.

With the data collected through employee interviews and continued feedback on existing programs, MCCCD's Employee Development program will continue to expand. Technology training is moving toward dual-platform software workshops, in-depth network training with a communication-based emphasis. Four-year apprenticeship programs for electricians, air conditioning technicians, and plumbers are in the offing. Management, supervisory, and clerical programs certified through the Arizona Department of Labor and provided with internal trainers are being planned. Team training and expansion of the current recognition programs will begin in the near future.

Listening, evaluating, and acting on employee comments and requests are foremost goals of the department of employee development. Input from internal experts is continually providing MCCCD with a rich array of professional and personal development programs. Keeping step with the quality improvement efforts throughout the district, the department of employee development strives to meet and exceed customer expectations.

PHYLLIS H. LEWIS is director of human resources at the University of Pennsylvania.

JAMIE C. CAVALIER is director of employee development at the Maricopa County Community College District.

ROSALYN HANTMAN is director of training and personnel development at Columbia University.

WILLIAM F. WAECHTER is vice chancellor of quality and employee development at the Maricopa County Community College District.

ALLAN H. YAMAKAWA is director of training and organization development at the University of Illinois at Chicago.

Some universities have responded to the need for leadership and staff development activities as the result of or as part of the quality improvement movement.

How Total Quality Management Initiatives Can Inspire Leadership

Sylvia Westerman

A leader decides what needs to be done and then tells people to do it. That's pretty much the definition that was in place for many years, certainly when I first went to work in the mid-1950s. But it doesn't sound right at all today, does it?

Let's try this one instead. "A leader is best when people barely know that he or she exists." Now that's more like it—that's the modern, 1990s way to think of a leader. Who said it? It's from the *Tao Te Ching* by sixth-century B.C. Chinese philosopher Lao Tzu, proving once again that there's nothing new under the sun. Many of the modern management principles embodied in the current movement known as Total Quality Management (TQM) are often touted as new and revolutionary when they are actually thoughtful, common-sense concepts that some managers have always practiced.

I say "some managers" because until recently the business world's leadership style was hierarchical, based primarily on a military model. In the 1950s and 1960s, all of us worked in a "don't ask questions, just do it" environment. Dictionaries of the period use the word *commanding* in the definitions of *leader*. That commanding style has been in place since the Industrial Revolution, imported to the United States from Europe, and seemed highly successful, especially during our post–World War II boom. Flaws in it did not become apparent until other countries, most notably Japan, became competitive and quality became an issue.

In 1979, an NBC documentary "If Japan Can, Why Can't We?" made the general public aware for the first time of the new management philosophies as the explanation for the so-called Japanese miracle. Adopted first by

NEW DIRECTIONS FOR HIGHER EDUCATION, no. 87, Fall 1994 © Jossey-Bass Publishers

manufacturing companies and the defense establishment, TQM has been modified over the past decade for use in service industries. A new concept of a leader as coach, cheerleader, and guide, as articulated in the various quality management philosophies promoted by W. Edwards Deming, Joseph Juran, Philip Crosby, and others, has emerged. Today, the first definition under *leader* in the *New Webster's Comprehensive Dictionary of the English Language* is "someone who acts as a guide." Here is how reporter John Case described a leader in the April 1993 issue of *Inc.* magazine: "The new approach redefines a CEO's job entirely. Instead of acting as commanding officer, issuing instructions, the CEO takes on twin roles. One is like that of a venture capitalist: dealing with investors, watching the numbers, allocating resources. The other is that of chief coach and coordinator, teaching people how to run their own show and making sure they're working from the same playbook" (Case, 1993, p. 93).

One way to think about leadership in the new management style is to consider those important and powerful graphic images we call organization charts. They are symbols that show us at a glance just how an institution thinks about its leadership. Hierarchical management charts show the leader at the top and everyone else in descending order. Another shows a redistribution of responsibility through a flattened organization, expressed by a squashed pyramid, still top-down. Picture a third kind of pyramid, this one turned on its side so that the "top" of the pyramid is on the left and everything else flows to the right. This is a graphic way to express many of the new leadership ideas. It reinforces the definition of a leader as coach and coordinator. In addition, it supports the concept of flow, of an organization receiving from its leadership its direction (mission), which then flows through the organization and on to its customers or beneficiaries.

This leads us to another message of the sideways pyramid. That long side of the triangle, now on the right, can be seen as the front line where the interface between employees and the outside world occurs. It is an immediate reminder that it is the employees below top management who are most often in contact with the outside world. This is the strongest reason to encourage their leadership abilities. You want those people to feel empowered to take the initiative and make appropriate decisions at their level. You also want them to feel so connected and responsible that they give full and timely feedback to the top leadership about what is really going on. That's their piece of the leadership pie. It's then up to the leader–coaches to use that feedback when they make decisions about the overall institution. This idea, in effect everyone a leader, does not mean chaos, just that there are different levels of leadership. Each employee can have a defined piece of the leadership pie and take responsibility within that area. The new management philosophies make this possible.

The question is how to begin the transformation of an institution. It is often said that TQM starts at the top, but I think we have to be careful with this, to be sure TQM does not go the way of Management By Objectives (MBO) and other horrors of the 1970s and 1980s that were forced on everyone, mandated by the boss. The beauty of TQM is that when employees understand its principles, they see the value to their own working life and will buy in. The only way for TQM to become a permanent way of business life is to get everyone involved and responsible. The common-sense aspects, the "I always thought we should do that" effect, make it possible for these new ideas to begin at a middle-management level.

Daniel Seymour, a business professor and administrator who has written widely in this field, posits three ways for TQM to start through an organization. One is the "trickle-down" method, with commitment at the top level; the second is the "bubble-up" method, with no need for initial top-level commitment; and the third is the "loose–tight" method, with some commitment at the top, pioneering units, and local champions (Seymour and Collett, 1991).

My own name for this third and most realistic method is the *ripple effect*. It's the way we have introduced TQM at Fordham, beginning in the Graduate Business School, with the support of the dean and faculty who teach TQM, and gradually spreading through the rest of the university. This method begins with the interest of a few upper and middle managers who learn about TQM by reading, attending seminars and conferences, and calling on outside consultants for in-house training. They begin to implement these new ideas and gradually the ideas spread. They are called local champions, a good description of the employees I referred to earlier who should have a piece of the leadership pie. This method seems particularly suited to academia. The vertical organization of educational institutions can make leadership within discrete units acceptable in a way it might not be in the corporate world.

I would like to describe my personal learning curve about TQM because I believe my experience is far from unique and demonstrates one of the strengths of the new management philosophy. Once employees understand its ideas and the usefulness of its tools, they will buy into rather than resist these new methods. In the corporate world, I had lived through the horrors of MBO, zero-based budgeting, and all the rest. The one characteristic they had in common was that top management brought them in and forced them down through the organization. Little attempt was made to generate enthusiasm among employees, and when a new management idea is forced on an institution, the amount of resistance it encounters almost guarantees failure. Employees do not cooperate; they figure out ways to get around the system. It is not good leadership if no one is following, if the enthusiasm is only among the leaders, not the led.

All this caused me to view any new management philosophy with great suspicion, so my eyes squinched up when I began hearing about TQM. One of my first insights came when I talked to Fordham faculty and discovered that many of the things I had either innovated as a manager or had thought should be done were part of this philosophy. I began to feel like the Molière character who was astonished to discover he had been speaking prose all his life.

What exactly is TQM and how does it encourage leadership? More particularly, what application does it have in the academic world? First, TQM is nothing less than a total change in the philosophy of management. Remember that the old style took a long time to develop and will take a long time to change, so this is not a quick fix. Second, some of the ideas and processes are not new. What is different is that now they have been pulled together under one umbrella and combined with a set of tools, especially the tools of statistics and process control.

Here are a few of the ideas that got my attention and caused me to nod in agreement. This, by the way, is a phenomenon all of us who speak on the subject notice: head-nodding in the audience, especially if the audience is made up of mid-level administrators. Often they know what is wrong with their institutions and have ideas of ways to fix things, but they have never been empowered to do so.

Employee Involvement

The more information employees have about what is going on and why they are doing what they are doing, the more able they are to take responsibility for decisions themselves. In my corporate life, other executives questioned why I was wasting my time giving my staff what they felt was more information than they needed to know. "Just tell them to do it," they said. But sharing information about goals can make each employee a leader, though clearly at different levels. If employees know why they are doing something and understand their part in the overall process, they will be able to make decisions. This does more than push responsibility down through the ranks of an organization, it pushes leadership down.

Blame the Process, Not the People

This idea really resonates with employees. Saying that when mistakes are made or a process is not working well, the process will be examined for its flaws rather than the employees being blamed, is a powerful leadership message. TQM offers techniques for that examination of processes.

Managing by Fact

This is the statistical underpinning of TQM, the idea that better management decisions are made on the basis of hard data, not anecdotes and gut feelings. An understanding of the principles of variation helps leaders make informed decisions about the need for change.

Customer Focus

This is nothing new, just treating customers as you yourself would like to be treated, the Golden Rule as a good management principle. The use of the word *customer* creates problems for academics, which I'll discuss later.

It is also important to emphasize what TQM is not. It is not just a set of tools or techniques. It is not a program, because a program has a beginning, a middle, and an end, and this implies you can finish and move on to something else. It is definitely not a thinly disguised new way of cost-saving or downsizing. Because there are many ideas, processes, and tools included under the TQM rubric, every organization must pick and choose among them to find what works.

This is especially true for the academic world, as Chaffee and Sherr point out in *Quality: Transforming Postsecondary Education* (1992): "First, TQM is a comprehensive philosophy, with principles and tools. Unlike many administrative innovations, TQM is not a recipe of ingredients and steps that must be followed slavishly to produce the intended result. Rather TQM is more like a well-equipped, well-stocked kitchen. TQM has the ingredients and the mechanisms of good management, from which organizations select those that suit their needs and purposes. A community college in Maine is free to make seafood dinners, while a university in Kansas fixes beef" (pp. 7–8).

The quality movement has only recently reached the academic world, but it is spreading rapidly. The business world has urged academia to catch up, and, of critical importance to education, most accrediting agencies have picked up the TQM language and concepts. Of course, an idea that comes to education from the business world is always suspect. The suggestion to academics that we are in "the education business" can provoke an outrage that seems to go all the way back to the medieval antagonisms between town and gown. Educators also have difficulty with the idea of "customers." Some faculty will never be enthusiastic and, in the spirit of academic freedom, there is no reason that they should be bothered or that the rest of us should worry about it. Some faculty are actually using TQM ideas and techniques under other names. Although I have used *TQM* as a label for these new management principles throughout this article, I should point out that a better phrase is now being used by the academic community: continuous quality improvement (CQI). For faculty especially, CQI can be more than just a different term for TQM. The phrase has a positive resonance because it speaks to a basic principle of education, the preparation of students not just for the present but for lifelong learning. Just take that concept one more step and think of the university and its administration as also experiencing lifelong learning, and you've arrived at continuous quality improvement.

As TQM begins on the administrative side and administrators treat faculty as customers, the faculty will notice that the quality of their own work life has improved and see the value of TQM. This was the way chosen by Oregon State University, one of the first to implement TQM and document its progress. As described in its two 1990 reports on its pilot program, Oregon State began with such areas as printing, physical plant, business affairs, and computer services (Coates, 1990). Of course, administrators themselves may go into shock at the idea of faculty as customers. I often startle an audience of administrators stating the two main administrative goals: improvement of the quality of life for students, in order to make learning easier, and improvement of the working environment for faculty, in order to make teaching and research easier.

The academic world has a very different mission from that of the corporate world, and will need a variety of creative leadership initiatives to shape the future use of this philosophy and its tools. It is all so new that I do not believe we need be discouraged by setbacks, just wary of plunging in too deeply too quickly. Ted Marchese, executive vice president of the American Association for Higher Education, points out:

> A few campus pioneers began their TQM effort in the eighties; the big wave of interest kicked in during the 1991–92 academic year; by now, it's hard to find a campus without a knot of people trying to implement the thing. On almost any campus, thin as the knowledge may yet be, people are already stoutly for Total Quality or deeply skeptical of it. What the quick-to-judge miss—what the early, triumphalist writing about TQM in higher education also misses—is that Total Quality is complicated, important, difficult to implement, and far from figured out. Contrary to the tool-driven, seven-step workshops that consultants are busily selling, we're years away from knowing what academic versions of TQM will appropriately look like. [Marchese, 1993, p. 10]

For instance, the vertical, pigeonholed nature of most educational institutions is often cited as a problem for the new management principles. Perhaps that vertical nature can be turned into an asset. It may be possible to work with rather than fight against it by encouraging leadership within discrete units of the institution. Mid-level managers as leaders must make sure their employees understand that these new methods will make life better for them as well as for the students and faculty. As E. W. Gore, Jr., writes in his chapter of *Continuous Quality Improvement,* "Just as the need for creating a common purpose, trust and a feeling of importance and participation were necessary in industry to effect permanent change, they are mandatory in education."

There are already a number of examples of middle-level leadership in quality management at universities and a literature of evidence about the opportunities and pitfalls in academia is emerging. The ones I know best and will describe are at Fordham, of course. You will note that in many cases middle managers learned on their own for a short time and then just started a project. This may not be the textbook way to approach major changes, but it is often the best, especially because we are trying to adapt processes from the business to the academic world. We can learn by doing, calling in expert assistance when we get stuck. A warning: whatever approach we take, there will be frustrations, false starts, and dead ends. This is not a short-term commitment and the academic world can understand this far better than the corporate world if we think of continuous improvement as lifelong learning.

Daniel Seymour (1993) describes what happened at Georgia Tech when one area, the Office of Minority Education Development, looked at the need to make Georgia Tech more appealing to women and minorities. The staff took a quality management course from a Georgia Tech professor who had worked with Deming and then just plunged in. After major changes in the department and the initiation of a continuous improvement process, Seymour says he found good reaction to the changes when he interviewed minority students, and mentions another important effect: "What captured the attention of many people at Tech has been the leadership of one office that decided to forgo long studies, leave the debates about CQI language and strategy to others, and to buckle down for some much-needed results" (p. 18).

Fordham's Graduate Business School has taught new quality management philosophies since 1986, so some faculty members were actually the first champions. Hearing about these concepts stimulated my interest and made me the first champion on the administrative side. With the support of the business school dean and the assistance of a faculty committee, I designed the 1991 annual faculty conference around the theme "How To Practice What We Teach." From this seminal event came several initiatives and more middle-management champions, some in parts of the university other than the Graduate Business School. Three examples:

• The Graduate Business School's Assistant Dean for Student Affairs, Lauren Mounty, formed a registration task force to improve that process. The group included faculty advisors, graduate students, and representatives from other university areas related to our registration operation. Incidentally, this task force ran into early snags because of a common problem— overeagerness. We tried to solve too long a list of problems and lost focus until we brought in another faculty member, one of our Deming masters, as a facilitator. The task force worked for more than a year and its initiatives continue to be implemented. Our registration packet is now rewritten before each mailing to improve its clarity and informativeness. Almost every student who has a registration problem, from not getting the desired class to a bursar hold, now gets an immediate phone call rather than the much slower mail notification. Says Dean Mounty, "I decided to use the phone, not mail, as the instrument of processing." Student satisfaction with improvements in the registration process is evident from the greatly reduced number of complaints and comments from student focus groups, always an important reality check.

I must point out that, like most universities, we had little or no hard data to use in taking some early corrective actions in these areas. Some solutions were so obvious when TQM techniques focused on them that we began changes and then instituted data collection, so we can continue to improve. Unlike an assembly-line that operates every day, many university systems such as registration operate only a few times a year. Waiting to collect enough data to be meaningful would be tantamount to abandoning the improvement effort.

• One member of the task force was the head of Fordham's computer operations (CIMS), Walter Weir. In an excellent illustration of the potential of middle-management initiative, Weir spread the word both up and down. He brought his staff to task force meetings and also communicated his enthusiasm to the vice president of planning and budget, who later attended our four-day TQM course for all senior university administrators. CIMS went on to form eight task forces to work with their internal customers and outside suppliers. When a fire caused all the university's computers to go down, CIMS staff and vendors had everything back up and running within twenty-four hours, a remarkable success story that Weir attributes to these initiatives (Weir and Westerman, 1992).

• When I marketed a four-day course, "Deming in Service Quality," taught by Fordham professor William Latzko, to corporate executives, I included five scholarships for Fordham university administrators. Those who attended were so enthusiastic that the university asked us to present a similar course for Fordham senior administrators. One attendee who became a champion, the dean of enrollment services for Fordham College, asked Dean Mounty and me to run a series of introductions to quality management that reached the entire staffs of recruiting, admissions, financial aid, bursar, and student housing.

These ripple effects are continuing and have the best chance of long-range success: because they were begun by mid-level management, they allow for a gradual buy-in at the middle and lower levels. In each case, a new initiative is prompted by enthusiasm for the processes and not by the belief that it's what the boss wants. On the other hand, it is not safe to assume that all employees will be eager to grasp this kind of empowerment when it is offered. Some may see more responsibility only as a reason to ask for more money or a new job title. Some may hyperventilate when confronted with permission to assume a leadership role and make decisions. Their behavior can be much like that of the Russian character played by Robin Williams in the movie *Moscow on the Hudson,* who fainted when he first encountered all the choices in an American supermarket.

The ripple effect method can be slow, exhausting, and sometimes discouraging, but I believe the results are more likely to be lasting. When in doubt, I always remember the tortoise and the hare.

References

Case, J. "A Company of Businesspeople." *INC. Magazine,* 1993, *15* (4), 79–93.

Chaffee, E. E., and Sherr, L. A. *Quality: Transforming Postsecondary Education,* Report Three, 1992 ASHE-ERIC Higher Education Reports. Washington, D.C.: George Washington University School of Education and Human Development, 1992.

Coates, L. E. *Implementing Total Quality Management in a University Setting.* Corvallis: Oregon State University, 1990.

Gore, E. W., Jr. "Total Quality Management in Education." In D. L. Hubbard (ed.), *Continuous Quality Improvement: Making the Transition to Education.* Maryville, Mo.: Prescott Publishing, 1993.

Marchese, T. "TQM: A Time for Ideas." *Change,* 1993, *25* (3), 10–13.

Seymour, D. "Quality on Campus: Three Institutions, Three Beginnings." *Change,* 1993, *25* (3),
14–27.

Seymour, D., and Collett, C. *Total Quality Management in Higher Education: A Critical Assessment.*
London: Methuen, GOAL/QPC, 1991.

Weir, W., and Westerman, S. "TQM: A Test of Fire." *Papers of Impro '92.* Wilton, Conn.: Juran
Institute, 1992.

*SYLVIA WESTERMAN is director of planning and new programs for the Graduate
School of Business Administration, Fordham University.*

Program evaluation is universal, but more persuasive measures of leadership development are needed to justify these programs in tough economic times.

Evaluating Leadership Development Programs

Sharon A. McDade

Should an institution evaluate the contributions of its leadership development efforts? Definitely. How do institutions evaluate their leadership development efforts? Some assess the need for programming, some survey individual leadership styles and status, and almost all evaluate their programs, but very few measure the actual leadership results.

How to evaluate leadership development and leadership culture is still an unexplored field, almost completely addressed through self-reported, qualitative, anecdotal commentary. It is perhaps because of the paucity of empirical evidence regarding leadership development and culture change that these programs are so vulnerable to budget cuts—it is easy to cut where there is no rigorous documentation of contribution to the improvement and validity of the institution. This chapter will explore the efforts that institutions make to evaluate need, programming, and results, and then offer observations on the problems of such evaluation.

Assessing Programming Need

Very few institutions conduct thorough needs analysis before embarking on leadership development activities. The need for leadership programming is rarely uncovered through needs analysis. Instead, the idea is most often advanced through an institutional champion (usually the president or chancellor) or by a committee interested in the general development of faculty or staff. As the profiles in this volume show, the idea of leadership programming

NEW DIRECTIONS FOR HIGHER EDUCATION, no. 87, Fall 1994 © Jossey-Bass Publishers

usually arises through a general, perceived need, not through an empirical organizational needs analysis.

Often, a mandate from the CEO or committee is verified and explored through a focused organizational needs analysis. For example, Columbia University conducted a needs assessment to more clearly evaluate the full range of training and professional development priorities across schools and administrative departments, with the goal that future programming was to be targeted to critical priorities based on the assessment results. More typically, however, leadership development programming is created because of a strongly held feeling of a need that should be addressed. Designed to fit this need, programming design is often heavily derived from national higher education or corporate leadership development program models, content, and format.

Surveying Individual Leadership Styles and Status

Many programs attempt to survey leadership styles or skills through the use of standardized tests. Use of the Myers–Briggs Type Indicator (MBTI) seems to be the most popular vehicle for accomplishing this, even though the MBTI really measures personality type, not leadership type. A wealth of research has matched the sixteen MBTI personality categories to people in various types of jobs. The leadership measurement is seen as the match to these job categories. Beyond this, the MBTI is popular because of its ability to categorize personality inclinations and thus provide a useful foundation for discussion about personality and, by derivation, leadership types. As a way to launch such discussions, the MBTI is an important vector for understanding the leadership culture of an institution and the leadership inclinations of its individual members.

Some programs use more specific individual evaluation tools. For example, the University of Illinois at Chicago program uses the Personal Profile and the Thomas–Kilmann Conflict Style Inventory to give insights into the role of personal style in creating interpersonal stress. These instruments are felt to develop understandings and clarify nomenclature for discussions of the role of individual style. In addition to the MBTI, the University of North Carolina at Greensboro uses the Fundamental Interpersonal Relations Orientation-Behavior (FIRO-B) and the Kirton Adaption-Innovation Inventory for the same reasons.

Virtually all of the instruments used in leadership programming survey leadership styles and orientations, but few, if any, actually measure leadership growth. Many instruments are based on specific personality-related theories. Others were originally designed to identify leadership characteristics as part of leadership selection processes and thus are based on particular concepts of leadership activity. Other instruments measure inspiration and influence, leadership behavior, and intellectual qualities of leaders. All of the major instruments are backed by impressive bodies of research documenting their usefulness, relationship to practice, and limitations (Clark and Clark, 1990). However, all of these instruments document leadership as it exists within a specific conceptual framework and at a specific moment at which the instrument is completed. The application to leadership development comes through the relationship of individual instruments to longitudinal studies about leaders.

Increasingly popular are 360-degree feedback mechanisms, such as those used by the Arizona State University Leadership Academy. These instruments capture feedback from peers, supervisors, and subordinates. The documentation is particularly useful to provide objective and comprehensive feedback as to how someone's leadership is perceived by others, and thus serves as an important foundation for discussion, learning, and subsequent development.

In whatever format, use of such leadership survey tools is an important component in many programs as a basis for individual understanding of behavior and leadership styles and as a foundation for discussion. For example, such assessment activities are the centerpiece of the ACCCA Annual Leadership Retreat, where the program participants spend two days in a relaxed environment learning about leadership through individual assessment.

Evaluating Programming

All programs described in this volume—indeed virtually all leadership development efforts, both campus-based and national—evaluate. All of the programs profiled in this volume consider themselves to be constantly under review through a variety of evaluation mechanisms. Such continual evaluation is felt to be necessary to sustain rigor and viability by incorporating feedback to make the program better.

Program evaluation is typically of three types: daily or event-specific, end-of-program review, and post-program evaluation. Daily or event-specific evaluations typically focus on program content, teaching, and format. Seattle Community College and Arizona State University use numerical rating scales and invite open-ended comments to evaluate each session. These evaluations give program coordinators immediate feedback on a variety of program issues. Despite such detailed evaluation, program directors cite difficulties in keeping programs fresh and closely related to personal and organizational needs.

All programs use some sort of end-of-experience evaluation, and many also collect reflections about the usefulness of the program at some point after the program completion. The difference is in how the evaluations are disseminated and collected, the specific information collected, the form of the data, and from whom the evaluation is collected. The CIC program conducts one of the most thorough program evaluations. Evaluation forms are mailed to all participants after each seminar and at the close of the fellowship year to gauge the success of the current activities and to solicit suggestions regarding future seminars. Campus liaisons are also asked for their evaluation after each seminar and for suggestions to improve quality. In support for funding renewal after four years, all fellows were contacted and asked to make judgments of the contribution of the program over time. The Arizona State University Leadership Academy collects evaluative data two weeks after completion of the program with the intent of capturing reflections about the long-term value of the program.

The programs at Kennesaw State employ steering committees made up of alumni who preview programs and suggest adjustments based on their own experiences, the changing needs of the institution, and documented responses from previous leadership classes. Inevitably, program directors, after extensive relationships with their programs, use personal observations to incorporate program changes as new issues and needs arise. Alumni evaluations at various intervals after the completion of the program are also common.

In general, the results of all of this programming feedback are positive. Personal commentary falls into five categories: individual development and growth through increased awareness of institutional functioning and specific job/role improvement; establishment of institutionwide networks and lasting friendships; enhancement of visibility to key decision makers who make future job selections; expanded knowledge of the institution, higher education issues, and community issues; and increased understanding of institutional decision-making processes and leaders. Institutional benefits most often cited include greater cooperation and collaboration among departments and units because of intra-institutional networks. Seattle Community College reported reduced tension and increased good humor.

Session- and issue-specific evaluation, whether positive, negative, or neutral, tends to be practical and applicable. Overall program evaluation tends to be positive but general, qualitative, personal, and anecdotal. These evaluations produce the participant comments that often appear later in brochures and advertising materials. Most programs reported that positive evaluations increased as time passed after the program. There also seems to be a perceived positive correlation over time from alumni who secured promotions and new jobs through program participation.

Measuring Leadership Development Results

Measuring leadership development results is a much more difficult task than simply evaluating satisfaction with programming because it requires documentation of changes in the perceptions, thinking patterns, behaviors, and actions of people over time. In reality, when we do take the time to measure leadership development results, we document leadership success, not leadership effectiveness. In this volume, only the ACCCA Mentoring Program cited follow-up measuring of developmental results through a doctoral dissertation by Majette-Daniels (1993) that surveyed career and psychosocial functions of the mentoring experience. The research especially supported the benefits of mentoring on psychosocial dimensions; career benefits were less strong, presumably because of the geographical and institutional dispersion of mentors and mentees.

Thus, evaluation tends to measure leadership orientations usually at the beginning of a developmental experience, as a snapshot in time. None of the programs comprehensively and consistently evaluate leadership effectiveness or improvement of effectiveness over time. The campus-based programs should not be faulted for such failure; none of the national higher education leadership programs and few corporate leadership development programs attempt such evaluation either. In this regard, program evaluation theory is still primitive, and treated as a second-class activity by researchers. The Center for Creative Leadership in Greensboro, North Carolina, is consistently challenging concepts of leadership evaluation, and thus making the greatest research strides in this regard.

Measuring leadership development involves an integration of a wide variety of personal development theories, intellectual growth concepts, learning styles, change process theory, risk-taking stratagems, and complex conceptualizations. Such complexity is very difficult to capture through number scales and other traditional empirical evaluation methods. For example, number scale data regarding satisfaction with a session are useful when compared against numbers for other sessions or against similar data from previous programs in that they indicate relative participant satisfaction and engagement. However, it is difficult to understand the meaning of a 3.87 in leadership development, effectiveness, and learning because there is no context for the number, nor is there any standardization for comparing such numbers.

Evaluation of leadership development must first speak to the program's—and, by extension, the institution's—values about leadership success and effectiveness. To be rigorous about such evaluation, there must first be a sorting out of the skills, behaviors, thinking patterns, and perceptions that the program is trying to promote; in other words, there must be a leadership paradigm and a philosophy of leadership development. However, even rigorous design born from such conceptualizations is complicated by the fact that leadership growth is not in a straight line; rather, it is roundabout that renders straightforward methods of evaluation inconclusive. Moreover, although the program may exhibit paradigm consistency, others in the institution may not conceive leadership in the same way. Views on leadership are highly skewed by values, assumptions about leadership and its development, weighting of the importance of traits and behaviors, and belief as to whether leaders are born or made.

Perhaps the cleanest method of evaluating leadership growth is to turn to the many available psychometric measures and standardized tests. However, these are usually complicated to administer, require special training for scoring, and are costly. More importantly, it is not always clear that such tests are directly applicable to what must be measured. Consequently, most organizations turn to home-grown, self-designed, and self-administered assessment tools. Thus, these issues become closely aligned to the current assessment movement that is trying to evaluate the effectiveness of college education.

A time-honored method of capturing change over time is through a pre- and posttest design. One way to accomplish this easily and inexpensively might be by repeating at a later time any survey instrument used to identify leadership orientations at an early point in the program. Changes in response to the instrument may indicate changes in leadership. Some commonly used instruments, such as the MBTI, may not be useful for this purpose because they are designed to capture a similar picture of a person each time the test is completed. Others lose their potency once participants understand the underlying theory of the instrument and can second-guess responses. Other, more specific leadership instruments may be helpful.

Participants themselves are the best source for documentation of change, but this takes time and participant cooperation to collect data in a systematic and comprehensive way. Stories are a particularly powerful documentation form—stories of critical incidents and how they were handled, about personal perceptions of change, about new initiatives and how they were handled. The goal is to collect journeys of leadership growth. Such stories can be collected through periodic paper instruments, journals, interviews, and focus groups. Because growth evolves over time, it would make sense to revisit participants at regular intervals for this evaluation—in essence, create a time-series evaluation format. The weakness of this strategy is that most people are poor observers of their own behavior, and this is particularly true as people are in the midst of the action. Also, adults tend to underestimate their own ability to grow and develop.

Another strategy is to collect less intensive data but from many sources. The 360-degree surveys have the most power for this purpose because they can capture changes in perceptions of leadership over time while providing multiple perspectives of the change. It would be helpful to collect views from mentors, supporters, supervisors, peers, members of committees on which the participant serves, subordinates, and so forth. A problem with this strategy is that if all of these evaluators are not trained in the concepts, objectives, theories, and language of the program, the result is idiosyncratic viewpoints instead of multiple viewpoints from a common conceptualization. One person's example of leadership effectiveness means nothing to someone else. A way to address this weakness would be to train some of these evaluation sources, such as supervisors, and then collect evaluations from these sources at regular intervals.

There are various other evaluation vehicles. Focus groups could bring members of a leadership development class together for reflection. This provides the benefit of comparing experiences among members that can spark introspection and provoke more instructive stories and observations than one person at a time might be able to provide. However, focus groups affect their members, creating new insights and inspiring new actions that cause the group to become an ongoing part of the program as opposed to simply an evaluation of the program. Another possibility is to follow a subpopulation of the program over time to trace how they grow in leadership effectiveness. Following such a subpopulation may make it more feasible to do intensive evaluation over time.

Yet another strategy would be to trace the growth of program participants as compared to that of a control group who did not participate in programming. Although this evaluation strategy would, in theory, provide the purest evaluation of the direct effectiveness of the impact of the program on leadership development, it is a difficult strategy to accomplish. Identifying a control group is a complex undertaking; one must match each participant with a nonparticipant of similar type. This strategy is confounded by the fact that the evaluation focus itself can change the control group. Moreover, it is difficult to justify keeping leadership development programming from one group while giving it to another if the goal is to train everyone for contribution to a culture of leadership.

To simplify the process, it might be wise to identify only a few specific areas for evaluation; for example, how someone improves in the effective leadership of pluralism. It is perhaps more feasible to keep checking on one or two dimensions of leadership growth with a large group of participants than to survey overall growth. What this strategy gains in depth of focus it loses in breadth.

Another variation would be to evaluate leadership growth indirectly through measurement of affiliated activities and changes. For example, it could be argued that improved leadership effectiveness is derived from an increased network of contacts through which a leader works and exerts influence. To this end, participants could be asked to detail their networks and relationships before and after the program so that these could be analyzed for such factors as number of people in the sphere of contact and the influence of the participant before and after. Another example could be analyzing the involvement level of the participant before and after the program. Is the participant more involved in campus, professional, and outside activities in leadership roles? How purposeful are participants in creating useful learning and growth opportunities for themselves after as compared with before the program?

There are many confounding effects on leadership development and thus on the evaluation of individual leadership growth that make evaluation complicated. These include the following:

Participants begin at different levels of intellectual and human development.
Leadership aspirations will probably be affected as a result of the intervention of the program. Participants may well aspire to different types or levels of leadership after the program than they would have conceived of before the program.
There is a halo effect inherent in participation. Expectations of leadership potential by those around the participants may change as a result of participation.
Much of leadership is about taking risks. Participants who are inspired by their program may attempt new risks as a result of empowerment felt through the program. But taking risks means more opportunities for failure as well as greater possibility of success. Others may see the failures without crediting them as noble experiments worthy of positive evaluation.

It is often difficult to separate management from leadership for evaluation purposes.

Evaluation of leadership styles is highly subjective.

It is virtually impossible to separate the actual and direct implications of the program from any other outside influences.

Other issues complicating evaluation are institutional and systemic, principally involving responsibility, time, money, and training. Program administrators are busy people, with other roles and responsibilities. Some are volunteers. Administration sometimes revolves from person to person and institution to institution. Operations are stretched thin, with little elasticity for comprehensive evaluation. Time is of the essence; thus, capturing what is easily recorded, as in daily, end-of-program, and postprogram evaluations makes sense. With meager funding, as much as possible is devoted to the participants program experience; evaluation is a secondary consideration. Rigorous evaluation usually requires training that administrators rarely have.

Leadership development is really the heart of the matter, but it is a very difficult task to measure—so difficult on so many dimensions that it is virtually impossible to do in any but the minimum way for the campus-based programs defined in this volume. Even the national (and presumably better-staffed and funded) programs rarely undertake such evaluation, so it is commendable for campus-based programs to attempt it at all.

Evaluation of Institutional Impact

A major shortcoming in evaluation is the inability to capture how the programs contribute to the overall life of the institution. Although documentation of contribution to individuals is generally accepted and supported, data regarding campus gains are even sketchier, harder to collect, and more difficult to analyze. The issues of institutional benefits are more variable and evaluated more through inference of other factors than through direct measurement. Other considerations mitigate measurement, such as whether or not there was consistent and equitable program follow-up, chemistry between mentor and mentee, and postprogram opportunities.

Such documentation is crucial for program funding. Virtually all of the leadership development programs described in this volume are supported through soft and discretionary monies. Thus, the programs must continually revalidate themselves to secure continued support in the face of changing campus leadership and uncertain economies. Many programs were launched with the support of special grant funds from outside sources. Once these grants ended, the programs had to justify their existence in the competition for scarce institutional funds. Evaluation data become crucial in this justification.

Conclusion

The issue of how to evaluate the effectiveness of leadership development efforts is closely tied to the question of what is leadership effectiveness. The very act of asking and looking at these issues changes things. Well-designed and comprehensive evaluation follow-up becomes part of the developmental intervention itself. The evaluation becomes part of the ongoing leadership intervention and reinforcement.

A major reason for evaluation is to provide feedback through which the program can be continually improved and more directly tied to the current and future needs of the institution. Certainly, simple programming evaluation appears to meet these goals. However, the fact that these data are not sufficient to argue for the long-term viability of these programs in the face of budget cutbacks suggests that additional and more rigorous evidence could be useful.

There is an old adage that the hardest things to measure are always the most important; the easiest things to measure are generally not as significant. This adage has great application to leadership development programming. It is easy to evaluate the programs themselves, and the results of these evaluations are helpful to their ongoing improvement. It is more difficult to evaluate program effectiveness, particularly in a subject with such wide interpretation as leadership effectiveness. Campus-based programs are in an excellent position to incorporate more vigorous evaluation into their design so that these issues can be explored.

References

Clark, K. E., and Clark, M. B. (eds.). *Measures of Leadership*. West Orange, N.J.: Leadership Library of America, 1990.

Majette-Daniels, B. "Mentoring Effectiveness in the Association of Community College Administrators (ACCCA) Mentoring Program." Ed.D. dissertation, University of San Francisco, 1993.

SHARON A. MCDADE is assistant professor of higher education and principal adviser of the higher education administration graduate programs at Teachers College, Columbia University.

Programming for leadership development may depend initially on the creativity of champions, but for the long term, such programming should be positioned in a unit that will nurture it long after its first proponents have left.

Implementing the Culture of Leadership

Phyllis H. Lewis

The history of internal leadership development activity on college and university campuses reveals a pattern of initial involvement by one or several inspired people. Programming of this sort requires the support if not the involvement of the highest-level administrators. Therefore, it is not surprising to find the initiator among that group. A number of the programs reviewed in this volume, for example, were inspired by the chief executive officer of their institution. President Betty Seigel of Kennesaw State College was the guiding force behind Leadership Kennesaw State College, a nationally recognized development program for faculty. Charles Kane, district chancellor for Seattle Community Colleges, and Thomas Meredith of Western Kentucky University were chiefly responsible for program development in their institutions. In some cases, the program was put together as implementation to directly support the objectives of the chief executive officer, such as Maricopa's staff development program, which supports chancellor Paul Eisner's vision of total quality.

Among those who have led efforts to build campus-based or consortium programs, many are alumni of the Harvard programs on leadership and management development and of the Higher Education Resource Services (HERS) Summer Institute for Women. Certainly the ideas and perspectives gained from participation in some of the highly regarded national institutes have germinated further development throughout the country. As established leaders on their own campuses, many alumni of these programs are already in a position to create initiatives to replicate for others their own experiences. For example, James Gallagher, president of the Philadelphia College of Textiles and Science, and Charles Kane of Seattle Community College both attended Harvard's Institute for Educational Management. Since then, both have supported the participation of many of their senior administrators in the Harvard programs; many others have participated in similar off-campus programs and institutes. President Gallagher's efforts have concentrated on helping his staff draw from those experiences to create an environment of teamwork and cooperation.

As long as the originator is the chief executive officer of the institution or some other high-ranking individual with the prestige and resources to make it happen, a program concept has a good chance of fruition. Even after its design stage, however, that individual must remain a visible champion or must have protégés and colleagues with strong commitment to keeping the program going. In fact, this volume has several examples of meritorious programs that were not continued or are on somewhat shaky footing because the key supporter left the university or no longer has influence over the program's continuation.

It is not always necessary for the "idea person" to be chief executive officer or in the top policy-making group. A creative staff person can surely do the job, but the key in this area, as in most new initiatives in a political environment, is garnering support from those with money and influence to carry forward an initial startup. Later on, the support must broaden to include those whom the program is meant to benefit.

The experience of human resource development programs at Boston College is a good example of how the work of a single charismatic individual with the right sphere of influence can set in motion major change to the institutional culture. In 1984, Alice Jeghelian, then director of affirmative action and assistant to the president, was considering ways to enhance the college's approach to diversity. In her role as the chief spokesperson for affirmative action on campus, she found herself frequently needing to make connections for others between the desired results and the reasons for them and to guide her clients individually along paths to reach good outcomes. She recognized, chiefly through her own experience, that better understandings about the legal framework for affirmative action and about supportive management behaviors could lead to more positive results, and she believed that others' attitudes could be shaped by improved knowledge.

In place since the late 1970s at Boston College was the Management Development Program. This twelve-week program was offered by invitation only to middle and senior administrators. That program had established a highly visible precedent for management development initiatives. Jeghelian had participated in the Management Development Program herself; although that format was not well-suited to her immediate goal of promoting better management skills, she believed that some form of management development program was needed. With support from the executive vice president, who had championed the long-standing senior-level Management Development Program, and from the director of human resources, Jeghelian conducted a needs assessment of the community. The questionnaire asked for feedback on the kinds of workshops and programs that would be useful. These preliminary efforts led to a decision by the director of human resources to create an office within the human resources organization to focus on human resource development. Alice Jeghelian became the first director of that office.

In the fall of 1985, the first programs—report writing, communication skills, and stress management—were offered. Other programs were quickly added. However, Jeghelian became concerned that the programs were not integrated with one another. In her words, the offerings were like a buffet, but she wanted to serve a full-course meal. Her approach was to take the array of offerings and design a core curriculum based on the information any new employee to Boston College needs to know. Everyone should understand, for example, the performance management system, policies on sexual and racial harassment, and the history and philosophy of the college. Supervisors should take courses in situational management, conflict resolution, interpersonal communication, and motivating employees.

When Jeghelian retired from her post in 1994, the human resource development office, now reporting to the vice president for human resources, could boast nearly forty different programs arranged under fifteen categories. Some of these pertain to leadership, supervision skills, financial and budget administration—all of which enhance professional performance; others relate to personal development. This entire curriculum, from which staff employees, supervisors, and some faculty have benefited for a decade, grew initially from the inspiration and commitment of one person who was able to secure and maintain campus support for her vision.

As the Boston College experience demonstrates, the leadership development initiative may begin as an add-on to the job responsibilities of some individuals. Eventually, however, it is likely to become by itself a wholly new unit or to affiliate as a new function with an existing unit. At Boston College, the program's home became the overall human resources unit. Among the programs reviewed in this volume, placement within the human resources function is by far the most common. Other units that sponsor these activities include the president's or chancellor's office, affirmative action, high-level academic offices, and continuing education.

There probably is no right office to house leadership programming, especially if the institution's environment truly supports a culture of leadership. However, during startup, especially, it is important for the sponsoring unit to have certain characteristics. Some of these are as follows:

Strong connection with the institution's planning process, including development of the mission. This feature is necessary so that the program initiative can be fully integrated with the work of the institution. As this volume has emphasized, in order for the development activity to be a truly worthy investment, nothing short of institutional culture change should be the aim. Such change can best be led by persons who have enlightened perspectives on how the institution's functional areas fit together to make the whole and who have access to the mechanisms for redirecting institutional energy.

Responsibility and capability for broad-scale programs directed toward at least one major population. Sometimes these programs begin as a broad staff development effort, with faculty participating on the basis of interest level and time availability. The reverse is also true; a program originally for faculty or senior administrators may be broadened to include staff.

Sensitivity to issues of both faculty and staff. Although the program may be directed to only one population, the relationship between faculty work and staff work and the connection of both to the institution's mission must be acknowledged. A training program that teaches customer service to staff, for example, should incorporate awareness about the important staff role in supporting retention efforts of faculty. Likewise, a program to help new faculty principal investigators deal with personnel issues must take into account faculty attitudes and staff needs.

Positive liaison with faculty governance structure and administrative processes. The unit initiating development activities, especially those that are tangential to academic interests, should search for allies among faculty governance leaders. If programs will be staffed partially by faculty contributors, those connections are especially important. At least, without strong connection to central administrative processes, the concept of programming has little likelihood of success.

Solid connections with resources in the outside community. Many of the programs described in this volume depend on resources from outside the institution. For example, staffing for a full range of programs may be done through the use of outside consultants, who may work on a fee basis, and speakers from government and nonprofit agencies, most of which do not charge fees. Thus the initiating unit should have strong networks with local talent pools.

This chapter has demonstrated that leadership programming sometimes is linked to the work of one or several forward-thinking individuals who themselves have the leadership to make it happen. As important as that initial creativity is, the personal charisma of one or several persons will have limited impact over the long term unless the newer thinking is somehow institutionalized. Leadership development programs cannot be merely an add-on, run as some specialized program with limited resources and visibility. On the other hand, it is not a good idea to make leadership development the business of every unit; that approach would lead to diffused responsibility for organized efforts. Programming for leadership development requires a place within the organizational framework that will ensure its eventual integration and influence within the campus culture long after its first proponents are no longer active in it.

The many programs reviewed in this volume demonstrate various approaches to leadership development for faculty, administrators, and staff. In

most cases, they represent important and far-reaching initiatives and entail significant resource allocation. There is evidence that these programs are regarded
seriously as a part of overall strategies to bring about improvements to their
institutions. In a few cases, in fact, participation in the development activity is
an expected part of the job performance. Some have attained such stature that
they have taken on an informal certifying function for members of certain
groups. Their alumni seem to carry with them some prestige and influence for
having participated in the program.

By approaching institutional change through development of human
resources, these programs are targeting the feature of higher education that
clearly represents its biggest budget ticket. Traditionally, however, this has been
the area of most neglect from a development standpoint. Proponents of these
programs are generally assertive about the need for greater commitment to
developing human resources. James Gallagher, president of Philadelphia College of Textiles and Science, notes that it is not enough to hire good people—
it is also necessary to invest in them. He points out that devoting money and
time to professional development helps increase the contribution faculty and
staff give back to the institution.

Colleges and universities cannot assume that those who have positions of
leadership really can lead. As one department chair at the University of Pennsylvania remarked recently, "One way we survive is to convince ourselves that
skills required for leading and managing people are intuitive; they are not!"
The expectations for performance in higher level positions are often quite different from the qualifications that actually appear on job postings. For example, negotiation skills, quite necessary for a dean, are not usually associated
with being a premier researcher and respected scholar. Greater emphasis on
developing academia's human resources may be one approach to solving the
extraordinary challenges facing higher education at the end of the twentieth
century.

One striking aspect of these leadership development activities, especially
the mature ones, is the degree to which they have become a way of doing business. Several programs reviewed in this volume illustrate important integration with principal functions. For example, Kennesaw State College's programs
for faculty and staff, which are nearing their ten-year mark with nearly 400
alumni, are regarded by leaders and those preparing to be leaders as necessary
steps for gaining understanding and enhancing one's credibility within the
organization. The extent of integration for Leadership for the '90s at Western
Kentucky University is the fact that it is required for all administrators and
managers who evaluate staff. Employee development activities at Maricopa
County Community College District essentially represent the preferred way of
carrying out the institutional mission through principles of total quality management and further support that principle by providing content knowledge
for meaningful employee involvement. Even without designing internal programs for leadership development, some schools are finding ways to integrate

available external institutes, conferences, and workshops into the business of the institution. Testimony of many in this volume demonstrates that these efforts to integrate learning experiences into the real work of the institution do pay off.

This focus on leadership development within the organization has brought the whole issue of professional and career development into focus as an institutional activity, not merely an individual concern. No doubt, these leadership programs do benefit individuals; sometimes, in fact, they are consciously directed to giving a career boost to underrepresented groups. An example of this approach is the BRIDGES program of the University of North Carolina at Chapel Hill, which was designed specifically to assist women to achieve professional growth. Similarly, the Penn State Administrators Fellows Program and the Program for Professional Enrichment at Eastern Illinois University admit only women and minorities. Most of the programs, however, have broad impact on diverse groups and do not specifically have a career development approach. Rather, the primary emphases are on bringing more contributors into the leadership circle and giving them the tools to do their current jobs better, including inspiring others in their units. The experience and networking opportunities gained from participation surely have great potential for enhancing careers, but those motives alone do not constitute the rationale for the institutional investment.

From the perspective of the individuals and groups served by development programs, such as those described here, the institutional mission may seem to have broadened. This reasoning would have faculty and staff among the group to benefit directly from the institution's educational services; in other words, the institution's own faculty and staff employees become students also. Whether or not that is an appropriate line of thinking is certainly debatable. Some institutional leaders and trustees may not easily see the value of including the workforce as a beneficiary of the educational mandate. Their question may be, Why are we investing in promoting the careers of staff when they are merely the tools to carry out the mission? Furthermore, staff who are privileged to attend such programs may regard these services as an employment right. Already, in fact, on some campuses, such as the University of Pennsylvania, staff organizations are calling for more programming directed to improving their professional growth. Where budgets are already very tight, it may seem hard to justify spending additional dollars on programming that does not address the basic mission of the institution.

What the initiatives described in this volume demonstrate, however, are some significant advantages of making staff development part of the overall educational purpose. Although it is indeed tempting to view our people—our human resources—in the same category as fiscal resources, machinery, and buildings, in truth, they are not the same. As our people learn how to learn better, the potential for them to give back to the organization is infinitely expandable. That point is especially true when learning grows out of shared experiences with colleagues and uses problem-solving methods that are compatible with one's own work environment. In short, the principal reason for investing in leadership development for faculty and staff is to bring about systemic change in the way faculty and staff view themselves in relation to their institution and in the way the institution views them. The result may very well be a more supportive and productive place for carrying out the important educational mission.

PHYLLIS H. LEWIS is director of human resources at the University of Pennsylvania.

Resources for program development are listed.

Annotated Bibliography on Leadership Development Programming in Higher Education

Henry A. Lewis

General Resources on Leadership in Higher Education

Bensimon, E. G., and Neumann, A. *Redesigning Collegiate Leadership: Teams and Teamwork in Higher Education.* Baltimore: Johns Hopkins University Press, 1993.

This study explores models of teamwork in higher education, taking into account leadership orientations of presidents and their executive officers. The authors examine how presidents and their designated team members work together; how team members perceive the quality of their working relationships; how presidents select, shape, and maintain particularly effective teams, and how teams address conflict and diversity of orientation among team members. Conclusions are based on interview data collected at fifteen participating institutions and also on the published research of others and the authors' experiences as participants in a variety of groups. Although the book speaks strongly to college and university presidents, other campus leaders may benefit who want to understand their own potential for contribution to a leadership team.

Birnbaum, R. *How Academic Leadership Works: Understanding Success and Failure in the College Presidency.* San Francisco: Jossey-Bass, 1992.

This book is about leadership in the academic community, or how a college president can make a difference in an institution's success in achieving its goals. The book is also about institutional renewal. Many leaders improve their colleges and leave them better than they found them; a few leaders do even more by helping college participants reaffirm their values, replenish their energy and commitment, and find satisfaction in their collective enterprise. This book is the result of a five-year longitudinal study—Institutional Leadership Project (ILP)—of how college and university presidents and other leaders interact and communicate, assess their own and others' effectiveness, establish goals, learn, transmit values, and make sense of the complex and dynamic organizations in which they work. Part I introduces the ideas of leadership that form the basis of the study and describes research findings. It proposes a definition of good leadership based on constituent support and assesses the extent to which institutional characteristics and the backgrounds, experiences, and styles of presidents relate to perceptions of presidents as good leaders. Part II considers the relationship between presidents and their several constituencies, how presidents are assessed by faculty, and ways in which leadership can be shared on the campus. A longitudinal portrait of three president career paths—the exemplary president, the model president, and the failed president—is provided. Suggestions are provided for improving institutional leadership.

Birnbaum, R. *How Colleges Work: The Cybernetics of Academic Organization Leadership.* San Francisco: Jossey-Bass, 1988.

Four models (bureaucratic, political, organized anarchy, and collegial) of academic leadership are discussed, along with their respective usefulness. The four models are synthesized and the best parts of each model form a new model of organization. The author illustrates how this new model can help academic leaders enhance their leadership competencies.

Brown, D. G., and others. "Preparing the Next Generation of Academic Leaders." *Liberal Education,* 1990, 76 (1), 32–41.

This article summarizes a two-day roundtable on preparing the next generation of academic leadership convened by the Association of American Colleges (AAC). Issues discussed relate to academic leadership: What is leadership? What can be done to enlarge the pool? Does the popular perception of a small pool reflect quantifiable and qualifiable reality? If the pool is diminished, can specific causes by identified? What can be done to expand and improve the pool of talent?

Cohen, M. D., and March, J. G. *Leadership and Ambiguity.* (2nd ed.) Boston: Harvard Business School Press, 1986.

This book examines some general ideas about leadership and ambiguity in the context of the American college president. This second edition adds short commentaries plus brief empirical addenda to the chapters on presidential activities and careers. Also included is an essay on administrative leadership.

Cunningham, J. J. *Black Administrators as Managers in Higher Education.* Washington, D.C.: ERIC Clearinghouse on Higher Education, Office of Education Research and Improvement, 1992. (ED 342 307)

The role of the black administrator has been important at black institutions and will become more important at predominantly white institutions as demographics and technology continue to change. Although black administrators have been given responsibility at predominantly white institutions, they have not been given the corresponding power. Given the changing demographics in higher education, institutions must spend effort and money on developing black and white administrators of the future. Programs are needed that develop administrators to rethink and expand their vision of the academic mission, renew their sense of intellectual confidence, overcome isolation, and deepen their understanding of leadership demands. It is becoming more difficult for senior administrators to rise from the faculty ranks. Future administrators must have training in many facets of institutional leadership and institutions must support the development of black administrators for positions of real authority.

Gorden, S. E., and Sindon, N. A. "Sources of Additional Information in the Area of Leadership Development." *NASPA Journal,* 1989, 27 (1), 80–88.

The authors of this special edition of *NASPA Journal* have discussed the importance of leadership education for both students and student personnel administrators on college and university campuses. The benefits of developing a more systematic and comprehensive approach to leadership are apparent. There are twenty-six citations (annotated) for books and articles dealing with the theory and implementation of leadership development. A section identifying opportunities for leadership development, such as the American Association for Higher Education, is also provided, along with additional sources to supplement the study of leadership and its relationship to the campus environment.

Green, M. F. "Developing Leadership: A Paradox in Academe." In R. H. Atwell and M. F. Green (eds.), *Academic Leaders as Managers.* New Directions for Higher Education, no. 36. San Francisco: Jossey-Bass, 1981.

Leadership and leadership development in academe pose a double-edged problem: the ambiguity of the educational enterprise—to provide students with an education—makes that enterprise hard to manage; the negative attitudes of educators toward the notion of managing education compound the basic problem. This negativism is rooted in a value system that reveres creativity and academic freedom and rejects the notion that colleges and universities produce quantifiable results. If colleges and universities are going to find creative solutions to the myriad of problems (declining enrollments, insufficient budgets, student consumers), serious attention must be paid to leadership development. Future leadership development programs must teach academic administrators not only how to lead faculty, but to develop the temperament and ability to manage people and money.

Green, M. "Investing in Leadership." *Liberal Education,* 1990, 76 (1), 6–13.

People are the most important resources in higher education, but higher education (in contrast to corporations) has paid little attention to developing its own leaders. Faculty who move into leadership roles identify more with their disciplines than with their institutions. Some of the prevailing attitudes for higher education's resistance to leadership development include the beliefs that anyone can be an administrator, that leadership development is too expensive and the return on investment is not worth it, that leadership is an art and not teachable, and that if you invest in people, they leave the institution for better jobs. Most academic leaders have had little or no preparation for their jobs; they learn as they go. Two types of leadership development programs can benefit academic administrators. Formal programs, such as the Harvard Institute for Educational Management, permit systematic exploration of a topic in a setting that encourages learning from peers. Informal programs, such as learning how other institutional operations function, provide leaders with a different perspective on their environments and their own jobs. The latter can be accomplished by mixing people from different areas within the institution through assignments that require individuals to meet colleagues and gain a better understanding of their operations.

Green, M. F. (ed.). *Leaders for a New Era: Strategies for Higher Education.* New York: American Council on Education and Macmillan, 1988.

Leadership is contextual. A leader is a product of his or her era, culture, and organizational setting. College and university administrators, faculty leaders, and department chairs face unique leadership challenges due to diminished resources and conflicting constituencies. The context of academic leadership is examined and potential leaders are recommended. New models are offered for the selection and training of leaders with different backgrounds, different styles, and different skills who will lead in different capacities.

Green, M. F., and McDade, S. A. *Investing in Higher Education: A Handbook of Leadership Development.* Washington, D.C.: American Council on Education, 1991.

Although colleges and universities play an active role in developing leaders for the corporate world, they give little attention to developing leaders for their own organizations. This book focuses on the reasons such development is important and the strategies for doing it. Part I describes the context of leadership development from institutional and individual perspectives, what institutions can hope to achieve by investing in leadership development, strategies for launching successful leadership development efforts, leadership development from the perspective of the individual, the tasks of leaders, and how leadership development can help people perform those tasks more effectively. Part

II focuses on the different groups within the institution, such as governing boards, presidents, vice presidents and senior administrators, academic deans, and department chairs, and describes the use of the team concept and performance evaluation as tools for leadership development. Part III focuses on implementing strategies: designing in-house efforts, using on-the-job-training, and selecting an external professional development program. The authors address how the institution and the individual can benefit from these experiences. The Appendix provides information on associations and brief descriptions of the national, statewide, and on-campus programs and practices listed at the end of various chapters. References follow each chapter.

McDade, S. A. *Leadership in Higher Education: Enhancing Skills Through Professional Development Programs*. Washington, D.C.: ERIC Clearinghouse on Higher Education, Office of Education Research and Improvement, 1988. (ED 301 144)

Many senior academic administrators of colleges and universities have had little management training; most prepared for academic careers in research and teaching. Because higher education continues to face difficult times, professional development programs can produce more visionary leaders needed to enhance the quality of a college or university. Professional development programs in higher education should address the following issues: career paths leading into administration, skills and knowledge required for executive positions, lessons gained from business and industry, and benefits and problems of participation. To be most effective, professional development experiences must be part of an integrated, organizational plan that links development activities with the actual tasks and responsibilities of the job.

McDade, S. A. "New Pathways in Leadership and Professional Development." In J. D. Fife and L. F. Goodchild (eds.), *Administration as a Profession*. New Directions for Higher Education, no. 76. San Francisco: Jossey-Bass, 1991.

This article explores the myth that all college and university officers follow traditional career ladders and education to senior leadership positions. The article argues that in the past decade, many administrators have augmented or substituted traditional career experiences and education with carefully designed and selected leadership and professional development experiences and programs. General programs by responsibility level are noted and discussed. The article argues for career-spanning leadership and professional development through the use of both on- and off-campus experiences.

McDade, S. A. "Planning for Career Improvement." In K. M. Moore and S. B. Twombly (eds.), *Administrative Careers and the Marketplace*. New Directions for Higher Education, no. 72. San Francisco: Jossey-Bass, 1990.

This article reviews issues relating to career improvement in terms of professional and leadership development for higher education administrators. It reviews on- and off-campus activities, particularly for administrators new to their positions. It particularly emphasizes the need for higher education administrators to plan their own leadership and professional development, and outlines strategies for doing so both on- and off-campus.

Pomrenke, V. "Team Leadership Development." In G. M. Hipps (ed.), *Effective Planned Change Strategies*. New Directions for Institutional Research, no. 33. San Francisco: Jossey-Bass, 1982.

This article describes two general models for bringing about change—the structural model and the people model. Team leadership and team building are viewed as people-oriented approaches to change that also affect the structure of an organization. Both targets of change—people and structure—should be approached in tandem.

Shavlik, D. L., and Touchton, J. G. "The New Agenda for Women Revisited." *Educational Record*, 1992, 73 (4), 47–55.

In 1989, Pearson and thirty-three other colleagues published *Educating the Majority: Women Challenge Tradition in Higher Education*. The book's central message is that educating women means more than admitting and graduating them, but understanding the culture of women. The book concluded with a set of recommendations for campuses to rethink the way they function relative to women. These recommendations were known as "The New Agenda for Women in Higher Education" and are revised in this article. These recommendations address women's employment in higher education, women's education, women's studies, campus climate, institutional commitment to women's needs and concerns through administrative and educational policies, attention to families and children, appreciation of diversity, athletics, and governance. One recommendation addresses the need for higher education to make leadership development and commitment to fostering women's leadership joint priorities. The demography of the contemporary world makes it more important than ever for leaders to be sensitive to the feelings, thoughts, and cultures of new and emerging constituencies.

Shoenberg, R. "Academic Leadership: Growing on Our Own." *Liberal Education*, 1990, 6 (1), 2–5.

The president of the faculty senate, the head of the employee union, and the president of a student organization have designated leadership positions; yet they get little formal help to prepare them to assume their roles. A leadership development plan should rest on two major goals: prestige and perspective. The former is a product of the way the program is managed, the latter its content. Prestige is created by the attention given the program, the involvement of all constituencies, the way the participants are chosen, the attractiveness of the opportunities afforded them, and the seriousness with which leaders are taken. Opportunities to learn from others who hold similar positions at other institutions or from those differently situated on one's own campus are some ways of gaining perspective. In addition, a leader must have knowledge of the basic facts of one's own campus—its history, the makeup of the student body and staff, fiscal constraints, and sources of income.

Wislocki-Goin, M. *The Tantric Proposition in Leadership Education: You Make Me Feel Like a Natural Woman.* Washington, D.C.: ERIC Clearinghouse on Higher Education, Office of Education Research and Improvement, 1993. (ED 362 085)

   This paper suggests that a male leadership model exists in higher education that oppresses and excludes women. Higher education must embrace the Eastern philosophy of the Tantric model, a shared model that views leadership as synergistic rather than separatist (males and females). The use of Eastern philosophy, quantum physics, and extant leadership theories are urged for the development of a new construct that is more interpersonal in concept. The Tantra is a Buddhist construct requiring that all living things be recognized as having intrinsic worth. Applying this approach to leadership brings a new way of defining leadership and how we teach it to others. Eighty-one references are included along with eight Tantric charts.

Specific Leadership Development Activities

Adrain, J. G., and Apps, J. W. "Kellogg Faculty Seminar: Enriching Academic Leadership in Adult/Continuing Education." *Innovative Higher Education,* 1990, *15* (1), 65–71.

   The Kellogg-funded Faculty Seminar on Future Directions in Continuing Education was a continuing professional development project for young assistant and associate professors of adult continuing education. Thirty-three early career faculty members focused on enriching their leadership roles within their academic departments and across the field of adult and continuing education. Seminar activities included residential conferences, career development projects, network and mentoring enterprises, database searching and electronic communications, and discussions on future directions in the field. Future directions in the field addressed such topics as research issues and training and development. With training and development, future interests were expressed in partnerships with the corporate world, defining professional knowledge, the uses of technology, and learning in the workplace.

American Council on Education. *A Review of the American Council on Education Fellows Program.* Washington, D.C.: American Council on Education, 1993.

   This report provides an evaluation of the American Council on Education Fellows Program by 147 of its past fellows and their mentors. This program is intended to develop the administrative skills of mid-career faculty and administrators. Each year, about thirty participants, under the guidance of a mentor, spend a year observing and participating in leadership, management, governance, and administration. Outcomes are reported in the following areas: achievement of objectives, development of leadership skills, acquisition of skills for management and administration, and benefits derived from the program for the institution. In addition, the report presents summaries of respondent evaluations for women, race and ethnicity, and of those involved in community colleges. Results suggest that the programming is achieving its goals; however, mentoring and the concerns of people of color and women are two major areas requiring additional attention.

Brightwell, D. S., and George, A. P. *A Group-Centered Leadership Model for Academic Departments.* Washington, D.C.: ERIC Clearinghouse on Higher Education, Office of Education Research and Improvement, 1989. (ED 317 130)

This group-centered organizational model was designed to allow faculty members in a large academic department the opportunity to participate in decisions concerning courses, curriculum, and programs. The model promotes the sharing of information, teamwork, and interdepartmental cooperation. The model is the result of a merger of two academic departments in which strict collective bargaining guidelines constrained all aspects of faculty work and roles. An organizational matrix clusters faculty across content areas and programs, each of which is represented by an academic coordinator and facilitator. At the start of a new academic year, department faculty identify and vote on goals to be achieved. The leadership to attain these goals is the responsibility of coordinators and facilitators working in pairs. The preparation of the coordinator or facilitator as leader is essential to the success of the model. Meetings are scheduled so that faculty may attend without conflict with regular teaching schedules.

Dieterich, D. *The Assessment of Need for Administrative Development on a University Campus.* Washington, D.C.: ERIC Clearinghouse on Higher Education, Office of Education Research and Improvement, 1986. (ED 265 764)

Professional development administrators at the University of Wisconsin–Stevens Point were assessed by survey questionnaire to determine which topics they had current knowledge about and which topics ($n = 89$) they needed to know more about to improve their administrative performance. Respondents ($n = 103$) indicated that they needed more development of the following: leadership skills, listening, reading quickly of good comprehension, writing effectively, delegating effectively, interpersonal skills, administrative roles, and stress management. A complete list of topics, rankings and importance scores, and the questionnaire are included.

Ebbers, L. H., Coyan, N., and Kelly, V. E. *LINC: Creating a Regional Consortium for Leadership Development.* Washington, D.C.: ERIC Clearinghouse on Higher Education, Office of Education Research and Improvement, 1992. (ED 348 089)

The Leadership Development for a New Century (LINC) began in 1989 as a consortium formed by the Iowa State University, the Iowa Association of Community College Trustees, and the Iowa Association of Community College Presidents. The mission of LINC was to increase the diversity of upper-level administrators at community colleges through developing and enhancing leadership styles of women and racial and ethnic minorities. This report provides an overview of the LINC program, including a discussion of the contributions of consortium members; LINC's coordination, funding, and organization; academic credit provided by LINC participation; LINC faculty and administration; and the LINC training environment. A LINC recruitment brochure is provided that includes goals, objectives, and institute activities. Other information consists of the 1991–1992 annual report, a two-page summary of a study evaluating LINC's effectiveness, a list of LINC participants, and a nomination form for participation in the LINC program.

Fly, E. H., and High, K. N. "Management Development at the University of Tennessee." *Business Officer,* Nov. 1984, pp. 32–34.

The University of Tennessee's Institute for Leadership Effectiveness is a week-long institute for mid- and senior-level administrators designed to provide insights and information concerning personal leadership styles and the principles and characteristics of organizations. Participants complete self-assessment instruments that provide insight into their communication, leadership, and conflict-handling styles. Through general sessions and small group interaction, participants address several topics including defining leadership, self-assessment, managing conflict, and campus culture. The institute provides ample time for informal discussions and interaction with peers and colleagues. (Editor's Note: This program is still viable.)

Haring-Hidore, M. "A Career Advancement Program for Women Administrators." *Journal of Career Development,* 1988, *14* (4), 279, 286.

The Career/Leadership Development Program was a pilot program designed to address the scarcity of women in administrative positions, especially in higher-level positions in higher education. The structure of the program includes a two-and-a-half day workshop with the following goals: high program accessibility to accommodate all interested female faculty and administrators, development of leadership skills and career advancement, career counseling sessions for each participant, and a one-day seminar training in fiscal matters.

Jurow, S. "Preparing Academic and Research Library Staff for the 1990s and Beyond." *Journal of Library Administration,* 1988, *17* (1), 5–17.

In an era of shrinking resources, academic libraries must make choices among the many services and programs they offer. Like the corporate sector, resource planning, career planning, and training and development can improve the effectiveness of service delivery and staff effectiveness. Satisfactory staff performance is no longer enough. Staff training programs are needed that focus on maintaining optimal performance levels through coaching skills, problem-solving skills, and sensitivity to organizational issues. The greatest challenge facing academic libraries, librarians, and staff is the ability to function in a changing environment. For libraries and library staff, this means being flexible and capable of shifting quickly in response to changing conditions.

Kimmich, C. M. "Trawling for Leaders: Campus Leadership Development at Brooklyn College." *Liberal Education,* 1992, 78 (5), 26–29.

The Brooklyn College leadership development program focuses on discovering leadership potential among faculty on campus who do not put themselves forward in ways that are conventionally regarded as leading. The program consists of five phases: emergence or identification—institutional settings where people are likely to demonstrate leadership; cultivation—encouraging self-identification of those who have leadership potential; classification—identifying the specific situations where leadership potential is demonstrated; authorization—placing identified talent in alternate situations for further development of leadership potential; and support—mentoring new leaders. To attract faculty interest, the program espouses three types of authority: substantive, or drawing on information and expertise that faculty members regard as part of their normal discipline; consultative, or requesting faculty to serve on consultative councils that address institutional issues; and indirect, or teaching faculty how to use their expertise in ways that may help the college function better.

Klisch, K. "Process and Outcomes: The Leadership Development Plan for Hood College." *Liberal Education,* 1992, 78 (5), 22–25.

The goal of the leadership development plan for Hood College is to increase opportunities for involvement in decision making and to improve communication among its various constituencies: faculty, students, and staff. A leadership development committee (LDC) of faculty members, students, and staff oversees this effort. Subgroups of the LDC (such as staff LDC) meet separately and seek advice from their respective constituencies. Because the Hood plan places a high priority on respect for the individual, staff from administrators to housekeepers communicate with the president to solve issues, faculty attend conferences and seminar programs such as those offered through the American Council on Education's Fellows Program, and students attend college-sponsored leadership programs and participate in decision making on matters related to student life.

McDade, S. A. "Leadership Development: A Key to the New Leadership Role of Student Affairs Professionals." *NASPA Journal,* 1989, 27 (1), 33–41.

Student personnel preparatory programs tend to concentrate on the counseling and human relations skills necessary for entry-level practitioners, but few institutions provide opportunities for leadership development of administrators, including student personnel officers. Before undertaking leadership development, it is first important to inventory the leadership capabilities needed for growth in a particular job and the next rung of responsibility. Leadership development activities are organized into the following: on-campus programs such as internships and job rotation; regional and national conventions such as attending national meetings, serving on committees and holding office in national organizations; seminars and workshops on executive education such as the Center for Creative Leadership; national institutes such as the Institute for Educational Management at Harvard University; and internships and fellowships such as the American Council on Education Fellows program.

Majette-Daniels, B. "Mentoring Effectiveness in the Association of California Community College Administrators (ACCCA) Mentoring Program." Unpublished doctoral dissertation, University of San Francisco, 1993.

The purpose of this study was to examine the effectiveness of ACCCA Mentor program as measured by the protégé and mentor perceptions. The program pairs mid- and senior-level administrators for a year-long mentoring experience designed to enhance career opportunities. The data, gathered through questionnaires, surveys, and interviews, were drawn through the participants' perceptions and expectations of their one-year dyadic mentorships between 1989 and 1992. Three instruments were used to conduct this study: the Mentoring Functions Questionnaire, Demographic Survey, and a structured interview protocol designed by the researcher. From the total population ($n = 145$), sixty-eight mentors and seventy-seven protégés representing sixty-six community colleges were identified as participants. Results suggested that protégés received more psychosocial support than strategic career-related assistance. Additional data from the interviews enhances this analysis.

Pauly, J. J. "Leading the University of Democracy." *Liberal Education,* 1992, *78* (5), 34–37.

Members of a leadership development team at the University of Tulsa focused on encouraging communication among nonacademic staff (secretaries, administrative assistants, clerical workers, technicians, and nonteaching professionals) through a series of structured group interviews. The results of this effort suggest that given the opportunity, nonacademic personnel can speak eloquently about their accomplishments and their problems. Many nonacademic personnel reported the lack of training and orientation given new employees. Many participants commented on how invigorating it was to simply meet with fellow employees and how this effort creates a more shared understanding of the institution's mission.

Roberts, J. "Leadership Programs: A Sampler." *Liberal Education,* 1990, *76* (1), 42–48.

The author, an editorial assistant for *Liberal Education,* has researched programs regularly offering training and experience to those specifically interested in playing leadership roles in colleges and universities. The American Council on Education (ACE) Fellows Program selects fellows through a rigorous national competition and helps identify and train promising education administrators. Fellows are nominated by their institution's chief executive officer, have five years of teaching or educational administrative experience, and come from administrative careers in higher education and academe. The ACE National Identification Program is designed to increase the number of women who serve as leaders in higher education. Women in mid- and senior-level positions in higher education are eligible to participate.

The National University Continuing Education Association Continuing Higher Education Leadership Project has a threefold mission: to develop data, materials, and programs to further the professional development of continuing higher educators; to examine significant public policy issues and their effects on lifelong learning; and to promote discussion among continuing educators, other higher education leaders, and representatives of the corporate and governmental issues. The Education Policy and Fellowship Program, sponsored by the Institute for Educational Leadership, is a year-long leadership development program designed for mid-career professionals who have demonstrated leadership in the field of education and related policy areas. The purpose of Harvard's Institute for Educational Management is to provide senior-level higher education administrators with leadership and management skills they need to guide their institutions into the next century. Participants must demonstrate that their authority and responsibilities affect institutional policy and that they have responsibilities that shape the future direction of their organization.

The Institutional Leadership Project at Teachers College, Columbia University, was a five-year study of academic leaders at a diverse sample of American higher education institutions. Results from that study take the form of a large number of useful publications. The Kellogg National Fellows Program's purpose is to expand the national pool of capable leaders. It is designed to allow the fellows to increase their skills and understanding of areas outside their chosen specialization so they can deal with complex leadership problems more effectively and creatively. The National Institute for Leadership Development assists women in two- and four-year colleges and universities in entering or advancing in administration. Bryn Mawr College's Summer Institute for Women in Higher Education Administration is a partnership between the college and Higher Education Resource Services and produces a summer institute to improve the status of women in higher education administration. The program provides women in the middle and upper levels of administration with management and governance skills.

Shoenberg, R. "Broadening the Base of Leadership: Eleven Campus Models for Leadership Development." *Liberal Education*, 1992, 78 (5), 38–54.

The author describes the Kellogg Foundation's funded project that provided support for the planning of leadership development initiatives at eleven colleges and universities. The program focuses of the following institutions of higher education are described: Allegheny Community College (includes everyone in institutional leadership), Baylor University (leadership development planning in a time of transition), Catonsville Community College (changing the community college mission to include leadership planning), Brooklyn College (indirect approach for developing new leaders), Gettysburg College (improving communication among campus constituencies), Hood College (leadership and personal development), Hunter College (workshop to explore leadership opportunities), Montgomery College (leadership development institute offering academic credit), Trinity University (student organizations offer formal leadership training), University of Tulsa (focus groups provide a sense of community), Wilkes University (leadership project unites diverse group in common effort).

Vaughan, G. B., and Gillet-Karam, R. "ACCLAIM: A Model for Leading the Community." *Community College Journal,* 1993, *63* (6), 20–23.

The article describes North Carolina State University's Academy for Community College Leadership Advancement, Innovation, and Modeling, a community-based program model. The ACCLAIM program consists of four major components: continuing education, the fellows program, information development and dissemination, and the involvement of university professors who teach the community college component in their university's higher education program. The purpose of the continuing education component is to provide an in-depth examination of community-based programming to eight pilot community colleges. The fellows program supplies the funding each year of the project for fifteen fellows to study on the North Carolina State University campus as full-time residential doctoral students. Information development and dissemination shares the experiences of ACCLAIM with community colleges and community leaders throughout the nation. The professors of higher education assist with course development and strengthen ties between universities and community colleges.

Whitaker, K. S. *Testing Our Values: Statements and Beliefs that Underlie Leadership Development.* Washington, D.C.: ERIC Clearinghouse on Higher Education, Office of Education Research and Improvement, 1991. (ED 339 107)

The policy and beliefs of a leadership development program at the University of Northern Colorado are described. The departmental philosophy for effective leadership is based on administrative experience to function within a diverse environment, achievement of a shared organizational vision, and continued learning. Seven belief statements and their rationale are described: human growth and development are lifelong pursuits; organizations are artifacts of a larger society; learning, teaching, and collegiality are fundamental activities of educational organizations; validated knowledge and active inquiry form the basis of practice; moral and ethical imperatives derive leadership behavior; leadership encompasses a learned set of knowledge, skills, and attitudes; and leaders effect positive change in individuals and organizations. A conclusion is that administrator preparation programs must develop a culture in which leaders understand how to create collegial learning environments that focus on growth of the total person.

Zimmerman, L. J., Radoye, V., and Itzkowitz, S. G. *Developing Leadership Skills: A Program Model and Its Impact.* Washington, D.C.: ERIC Clearinghouse on Higher Education, Office of Education Research and Improvement, 1991. (ED 336 671)

Leadership development is essential to the future of the student affairs profession and colleges and universities must fund participation in professional development programs. Wayne State University provides learning opportunities for professional development on campus. Professional staff are encouraged to participate in professional associations, workshops, and conferences, and to develop a strong peer support system on the campus. Evaluation of this effort was accomplished with a survey administered to all individuals eligible to participate in this program. Preliminary results suggest greater job satisfaction, expanded leadership roles, increased productivity, and an enhanced sense of professional identity. An indirect result has been expanded services to students. The university and the students it serves can only benefit by promoting, supporting, and requiring professional development among student development professionals.

HENRY A. LEWIS is lecturer in the department of management and marketing, Bryan School of Business and Economics, University of North Carolina at Greensboro, and a feedback consultant for the Center for Creative Leadership in Greensboro.

APPENDIX: RESOURCE CONTACTS

Editors

Sharon A. McDade, Assistant Professor, Department of Higher and Adult Education and Principal Adviser, Higher Education Administration Graduate Programs, Teachers College, Columbia University, 525 West 120th Street, Box 101, New York, N.Y. 10027. Phone (212) 678-3750; fax (212) 678-4048; E-mail sam44@columbia.edu.

Phyllis H. Lewis, Director of Human Resources, University of Pennsylvania, 527A 3401 Walnut Street, Philadelphia, PA 19104-6228. Phone (215) 898-6019; fax (215) 898-0403.

Chapter Two

Anne K. Ard, Senior Diversity Planning Analyst, Pennsylvania State University, 314 Orange Building, University Park, PA 16802. Phone (814) 863-7890; fax (814) 863-8218.

Chapter Three

James P. Gallagher, President, Philadelphia College of Textiles and Science, Schoolhouse Lane & Henry Avenue, Philadelphia, PA 19144. Phone (215) 951-2970.

Chapter Four

Laura M. Fino, Leadership Academy Coordinator, Staff Development, Arizona State University, Box 871403, Tempe, AZ 85287-1403. Phone (602) 965-2852; fax (602) 965-0928.

Julie Y. Hungar, Vice Chancellor for Education and Planning, Seattle Community College District, 1500 Harvard, Seattle, WA 98122. Phone (206) 587-4101; fax (206) 587-3894.

William H. Wallace, Jr., Director of Human Resources, Kennesaw State College, P. O. Box 444, Marietta, GA 30061. Phone (404) 423-6030; fax (404) 423-6570.

Richard F. Welch, Interim Director, Center for Excellence in Teaching and Learning, Kennesaw State College, P. O. Box 444, Marietta, GA 30061. Phone (404) 423-6410; fax (404) 423-6740.

Wally Skiba, Associate Director, Human Resource Services, 307 Service Building, University of Kentucky, Lexington, KY 40506-0005. Phone (606) 257-6314; fax (606) 323-1075.

Daniel W. Wheeler, Coordinator, Office of Professional and Organizational Development, University of Nebraska-Lincoln, P .O. Box 830904, Lincoln, NE 68583-0904. Phone (402) 472-5558; fax (402) 472-6799.

Rachel M. Davies, Program Director, BRIDGES, Division of Continuing Education, University of North Carolina at Chapel Hill, Campus Box 1020, The Friday Center, Chapel Hill, NC 27599-1020. Phone (919) 962-1124; fax (919) 962-2061.

Sandra Webb, Director of Continuing Education, Western Kentucky University, Bowling Green, KY 42101. Phone (502) 745-1912; fax (502) 745-1911.

Chapter Five

Kenneth E. Anderson, Committee for Institutional Cooperation (Big 10 Plus University of Chicago and Pennsylvania State University) Academic Leadership Program, Office of the Vice Chancellor for Academic Affairs, Swanlund Administration Building, 601 East John Street, Champaign, IL 61820. Phone (217) 333-8846.

Frances L. White, Coordinator, The Association of California Community College Administrators Mentor Program, Laney College, 900 Fallon Street, Oakland, CA 94607. Phone (510) 464-3221.

Maria Santos, California State University System Executive Leadership Development Program, Statewide Dean, Affirmative Action, The California State University, Office of the Chancellor, Suite 222, 400 Golden Shore, Long Beach, CA 90802-4275. Phone (310) 985-2660.

Chapter Six

Jamie C. Cavalier, Director, Employee Development, Maricopa Community Colleges, 2411 W. 14th Street, Tempe, AZ 85281-6941. Phone (602) 731-8283; fax (602) 731-8235.

Allan H. Yamakawa, Director, Training and Organization Development (M/C 823), University of Illinois at Chicago, 1140 South Paulina Street, Chicago, IL 60612-7216. Phone (312) 996-3504; fax (312) 996-0599.

Rosalyn F. Hantman, Director of Training & Development, Columbia University, 475 Riverside Drive, Room 516, New York, NY 10115. Phone (212) 870-2100; fax (212) 870-2887.

Anora R. Robbins, Acting Associate Vice Chancellor for Human Resources, The University of North Carolina at Greensboro, 1100 W. Market Street, Greensboro, NC 27412. Phone (910) 334-5009; fax (910) 334-5585.

Chapter Seven

Sylvia Westerman, Director of Planning and New Programs, Graduate School of Business Administration, Fordham University, 113 West 60th Street, New York, N.Y. 10023. Phone: (212) 636-6167.

INDEX

ORDERING INFORMATION

NEW DIRECTIONS FOR HIGHER EDUCATION is a series of paperback books that provides timely information and authoritative advice about major issues and administrative problems confronting every institution. Books in the series are published quarterly in Spring, Summer, Fall, and Winter and are available for purchase by subscription and individually.

SUBSCRIPTIONS for 1994 cost $47.00 for individuals (a savings of 25 percent over single-copy prices) and $62.00 for institutions, agencies, and libraries. Please do not send institutional checks for personal subscriptions. Standing orders are accepted.

SINGLE COPIES cost $16.95 when payment accompanies order. (California, New Jersey, New York, and Washington, D.C., residents please include appropriate sales tax.) Billed orders will be charged postage and handling.

DISCOUNTS FOR QUANTITY ORDERS are available. Please write to the address below for information.

ALL ORDERS must include either the name of an individual or an official purchase order number. Please submit your order as follows:
   Subscriptions: specify series and year subscription is to begin
   Single copies: include individual title code (such as HE82)

MAIL ALL ORDERS TO:
   Jossey-Bass Publishers
   350 Sansome Street
   San Francisco, California 94104-1342

FOR SUBSCRIPTION SALES OUTSIDE OF THE UNITED STATES, contact any international
   subscription agency or Jossey-Bass directly.

Statement of Ownership, Management and Circulation

(Required by 39 U.S.C. 3685)

1A. Title of Publication	1B. PUBLICATION NO.	2. Date of Filing
NEW DIRECTIONS FOR HIGHER EDUCATION	0 7 7 1 0 5 6 0	9/26/94

3. Frequency of Issue	3A. No. of Issues Published Annually	3B. Annual Subscription Price
Quarterly	Four (4)	$47.00 (personal) $62.00 (institution)

4. Complete Mailing Address of Known Office of Publication (Street, City, County, State and ZIP+4 Code) (Not printers)

350 Sansome Street, 5th Flr, San Francisco, CA 94104-1342 (San Francisco Cnt)

5. Complete Mailing Address of the Headquarters of General Business Offices of the Publisher (Not printer)

(above address)

6. Full Names and Complete Mailing Address of Publisher, Editor, and Managing Editor (This item MUST NOT be blank)

Publisher (Name and Complete Mailing Address)

Jossey-Bass Inc., Publishers (above address)

Editor (Name and Complete Mailing Address)

Martin Kramer, 2807 Shasta Road, Berkeley, CA 94708-2011

Managing Editor (Name and Complete Mailing Address)

Lynn D. Luckow, President, Jossey-Bass Inc., Publishers (address above)

7. Owner (If owned by a corporation, its name and address must be stated and also immediately thereunder the names and addresses of stockholders owning or holding 1 percent or more of total amount of stock. If not owned by a corporation, the names and addresses of the individual owners must be given. If owned by a partnership or other unincorporated firm, its name and address, as well as that of each individual must be given. If the publication is published by a nonprofit organization, its name and address must be stated.) (Item must be completed.)

Full Name	Complete Mailing Address
SIMON & SCHUSTER	PO Box 1172 Englewood Cliffs, NJ 07632-1172

8. Known Bondholders, Mortgagees, and Other Security Holders Owning or Holding 1 Percent or More of Total Amount of Bonds, Mortgages or Other Securities (If there are none, so state)

Full Name	Complete Mailing Address
SAME AS ABOVE	SAME AS ABOVE

9. For Completion by Nonprofit Organizations Authorized To Mail at Special Rates (DMM Section 424.12 only) The purpose, function, and nonprofit status of this organization and the exempt status for Federal income tax purposes (Check one)

☐ (1) Has Not Changed During Preceding 12 Months ☐ (2) Has Changed During Preceding 12 Months (If changed, publisher must submit explanation of change with this statement)

10.	Extent and Nature of Circulation	Average No. Copies Each Issue During Preceding 12 Months	Actual No. Copies of Single Issue Published Nearest to Filing Date
A.	Total No. Copies (Net Press Run)	2,754	2,973
B.	Paid and/or Requested Circulation 1. Sales through dealers and carriers, street vendors and counter sales	755	174
	2. Mail Subscription (Paid and/or requested)	1,106	1,082
C.	Total Paid and/or Requested Circulation (Sum of 10B1 and 10B2)	1,861	1,256
D.	Free Distribution by Mail, Carrier or Other Means Samples, Complimentary, and Other Free Copies	66	66
E.	Total Distribution (Sum of C and D)	1,927	1,322
F.	Copies Not Distributed 1. Office use, left over, unaccounted, spoiled after printing	827	1,651
	2. Return from News Agents	0	0
G.	TOTAL (Sum of E, F1 and 2—should equal net press run shown in A)	2,754	2,973

11. I certify that the statements made by me above are correct and complete

Signature and Title of Editor, Publisher, Business Manager, or Owner

Larry Ishii Vice President

PS Form 3526, January 1991